D0984595

An Annotated Critical Bibliography
of James Joyce

An Annotated Critical Bibliography of James Joyce

Thomas F. Staley

*Professor of English and Director of the
Harry Ransom Humanities Research Center
University of Texas, Austin*

St. Martin's Press
New York

First published in the United States of America in 1989

Printed in Great Britain

ISBN 0-312-01963-7

Library of Congress Cataloging-in-Publication Data
Staley, Thomas F.
  An annotated critical bibliography of James Joyce /
Thomas F. Staley.
      p.   cm.
  Bibliography: p.
  Includes index.
  ISBN 0-312-01963-7 : $35.00 (est.)
  1. Joyce, James, 1882-1941—Bibliography.   I. Title.
Z8458.1.S73   1989
[PR6019.09]   88-39097
016.823'912—dc19   CIP

Contents

Advice to the Reader

The weight of Joyce scholarship is indeed a heavy one. This work is intended to lighten the burden. For the many readers of Joyce, from beginning students to non-specialist, advanced readers, this work is intended as a guide. Besides offering commentary on individual critical studies, read straight through, the annotations are intended to trace the directions and developments in Joyce scholarship through the mid-1980s.

Joyce's work has attracted the attention of some of the finest literary intelligences of the century, and many of their studies are recorded in these pages. There is also much that has been written about Joyce that deserves to be left unread and this selection acknowledges that by neglect. In many instances, however, there are studies with which I am in deep disagreement, and a few which are, I believe, provocatively wrong. These are included, for the most part, without rancour for the reader to make separate judgements.

This selection makes no pretence at completeness, but at the same time it attempts to be thorough in that the major and influential works are covered. There are other bibliographies that strive for comprehensive listings and are certainly less directive. This work, like others in the Series, is not primarily a work of bibliographical scholarship but of criticism. Robert Deming's secondary bibliography (1977), for example, lists over 5,500 studies through 1973, and Thomas Rice's excellent *James Joyce: A Guide to Research* includes 1,967 entries through 1981. My inclusions lean far more heavily toward books than articles except in the case of the earlier works. This is not merely arbitrary, for, with important exceptions that are listed, many of these essays grew into larger studies. As a rule, highly specialized articles which cover narrow areas are not included.

Since this is a selective guide and is arranged chronologically within its divisions, some works were chosen primarily because they are historically representative and reflect particular stages in the evolution of Joyce criticism. The trail of Joyce criticism is hardly a straight one and it is important to see bends and turns as they come along. Foreign language work that has not been translated is included only in rare instances such as when the work's importance dictates inclusion, a comparable study is not available in English, or the work contains a significant bibliography.

The entries are described in varying detail, but these annotations are evaluative in many instances. Some entries, because of what I believe to be their importance and influence, are discussed extensively, and an effort is frequently made to take into account the critical context as well. So, both the selection process and the annotations themselves reflect my opinions gleaned from working within this subject for over twenty-five years both as a critic and as editor of the *James Joyce Quarterly*, now in its twenty-sixth year.

As the Contents shows, this bibliography is arranged in ten sections with appropriate subsections where necessary for ease of use. At the beginning of many of the sections there is a brief statement of explanation or suggestions for further reference as well as a selection of helpful cross-listings. These cross-listings amplify the bibliography; they are likewise selective, intended to suggest other entries which are especially pertinent to the work covered in the section. Many of the entries cover material beyond the section where they are listed; therefore, this cross-listing was needed, but the intention was to be helpful, not exhaustive. A word is required about collections of essays, of which there are many. The collection is listed and the essays, however diverse, and, however thoroughly discussed, are usually described only under the single entry. For example, *James Joyce Today* (D32) appears in the general section and the essays in the volume are mentioned under this entry, but a reference to this volume will appear in the cross-listings at the beginning of a section, say *Ulysses*, to refer to the essay from the volume that deals with *Ulysses* specifically. In addition to the cross-listings at the beginning of many sections, cross-listings are also used selectively within annotations. These appear primarily in annotations for articles that have been reprinted in essay collections and indicate the collection in which the article can be found. The bibliography concludes with an index of contributors.

A work such as this calls on the achievement and support of a large community of scholars, and over the years many have been generous. While certainly not always harmonious, the Joyce community has been a cooperative and open one.

Four people have contributed greatly to this work. Bernice Coyle typed this manuscript faultlessly as she has so many of my other manuscripts. Scott Simpkins helped me with research at the early stages of work. Joan Seay served as editorial assistant and worked on bibliographical matters and cross-listings. Michael Warner worked in innumerable ways to bring this work to fruition and helped me decide on many of the later inclusions. Many were the hours of discussion, debate, and clarification regarding inclusion and exclusion, and annotations themselves in a few entries. The errors, of course, of both judgement and fact are my responsibility.

The reward an undertaking such as this brings is the pleasure of retrospection, recalling one's reactions to so many works with which one has lived for a long time and, in the case of the later studies, seeing how that body of work has grown and changed with new avenues opened and older discoveries reinforced or altered. Joyce's work has absorbed critics and scholars as much as any writer of the century, and as is the case with any great artist, this absorption with his work is a testimony to Joyce's influence and genius.

Thomas F. Staley
25 April 1988

Bibliography

In addition to the bibliographies and bibliographical essays listed in this section, consult the annual bibliography published by the Modern Language Association of America and supplemented each year by Alan Cohn in the *James Joyce Quarterly*. This should be done routinely after 1986, although several books and articles published in 1987 have been included in this volume.
See also: D98 and F6.

A1   McLuhan, H. Marshall
      "A Survey of Joyce Criticism", *Renascence*, 4 (1951), 12–18

      A general look at Joyce criticism through the 1940s that, read in retrospect, gives an interesting perspective on the early formal response to Joyce's work.

A2   Slocum, John J., and Herbert Cahoon, eds
      A BIBLIOGRAPHY OF JAMES JOYCE (1882–1941) (New Haven: Yale University Press, 1953; rpt Westport, Conn.: Greenwood Press, 1971)

      A distinguished primary bibliography which covers material to 1950, with occasional subsequent additions. Given the curious and complex history of Joyce's published work, this bibliography is an important document in modern literary history in addition to being a valuable literary tool. In spite of its comprehensiveness, the book omits several publications prior to 1950. Besides omissions, further variants have also been discovered in several editions, but it remains to be determined whether these are true variants or are merely freak copies. Because of the relatively large number of primary works published after 1950, there is also a serious need for a new primary bibliography accounting for later posthumous publications and editions.

A3   Connolly, Thomas E., comp.
      THE PERSONAL LIBRARY OF JAMES JOYCE: A DESCRIPTIVE BIBLIOGRAPHY (1955; 2nd edn, Buffalo, N.Y.: University Bookstore, University of Buffalo, 1957)

Catalogues the working library Joyce had during the winter of 1938–39. Included in the books, periodicals and pamphlets are works that range from Joyce's school-days to various foreign language aids used for *Finnegans Wake*. This collection, housed at the Lockwood Memorial Library at the University of Buffalo, also contains notebooks, manuscripts and letters of Joyce.

A4   Adams, Robert Martin
"The Bent Knife Blade: Joyce in the 1960s", *Partisan Review*, 29 (1962), 507–18

Though not a bibliographical essay, this article provides a broad critical perspective from which the scholar can view Joyce's art in light of the contemporary critical and cultural climate.

A5   Cohn, Alan M., and Richard M. Kain, comps
"Supplemental JJ Checklist 1962" (now "Current JJ Checklist"), *James Joyce Quarterly*, 1 (1964–)

Cohn's checklist appears each year in the *James Joyce Quarterly* as a supplement to the annual *MLA International Bibliography*. Cohn's bibliographies are far more extensive then the MLA annuals, for he not only lists omissions of secondary materials but also lists book reviews and new primary material, new translations, recordings, tapes, musical settings, films, and dissertations. This is an accurate, up-to-date bibliographical tool and a valuable source for current research.

A6   Deming, Robert H., ed.
A BIBLIOGRAPHY OF JAMES JOYCE STUDIES (1964; 2nd edn, Boston: Hall, 1977)

Deming's second edition incorporates the listings from the first edition that covered the years to 1961 with new entries to bring the coverage up to 1973. Deming has added about 770 items from the pre-1961 period that were not included in his first edition. He eliminates nearly all the annotations provided for entries in the first edition, noting that "the sacrifice of this information should be compensated for by the greater completeness of this edition." Omissions in Deming's work include books of European criticism that deal in passing with Joyce and introductions to editions, such as James S. Atherton's introduction and notes to the Heinemann edition of *A Portrait* (1964). Deming's classification and arrangement of material is generally clear and helpful. The work is accurate and the general principles of inclusion and classification are sound.

A7 Cohn, Alan M.
"Joyce Bibliographies: A Survey", *American Book Collector*, 15:10 (1965), 11–16

This work sorts out a number of secondary bibliographies and checklists prior to 1960, showing their relations to one another. Primary bibliographies are also included.

A8 Beebe, Maurice, Phillip Herring, and A. Walton Litz, comps
"Criticism of James Joyce: A Selected Checklist", *Modern Fiction Studies*, 15 (1969), 105–82

An excellent selective bibliography of earlier secondary Joyce material. This checklist developed out of the 1958 *MFS* checklist and follows the same general outline. It re-edits, updates and pulls together previous supplements: the 1958 checklist updated by Beebe & Litz, in *La Revue des Lettres Modernes* (1959/1960); and a later supplement for the period of 1959 to early 1964 by Cohn and Herring, also in *La Revue* (1965). In spite of its length (over seventy-five pages), the compilers note that their checklist "is a selection from the vast amount of material that might have been included".

A9 Füger, Wilhelm, ed.
JAMES JOYCE'S *PORTRAIT*: DAS *JUGENDBILDNIS* IM LICHTE NEURER DEUTSCHER FORSCHUNG (Munich: Wilhelm Goldmann Verlag, 1972)

The most complete bibliography of *A Portrait*. Lists 455 secondary items and offers as well a special section listing translations of *A Portrait*.

A10 White, William
"James Joyce", *New Cambridge Bibliography of English*

Literature, vol 4 (Cambridge: Cambridge University Press, 1972), pp. 444–71

Offers a good general coverage of both primary and secondary material through 1969.

A11   Litz, A. Walton
"Joyce", THE ENGLISH NOVEL: SELECT BIBLIO-GRAPHICAL GUIDES, ed. A. E. Dyson (London: Oxford University Press, 1974), pp. 349–69

Although not exhaustive, a good bibliographical survey that covers the best studies and places them in the perspective of Joyce's changing critical reputation.

A12   Staley, Thomas F.
"James Joyce", ANGLO-IRISH LITERATURE: A REVIEW OF RESEARCH, ed. Richard J. Finneran (New York: Modern Language Association, 1976), pp. 366–435

An extended bibliographical essay which traces Joyce scholarship in an historical narrative. Both primary and secondary works are included in a scheme of topical classification and critical annotation. Works are treated in depth according to their importance in the field. In addition, critical issues and conflicts within Joyce scholarship are explored. This essay gives a guide to scholarly resources to 1975.

A13   Benstock, Bernard
"The James Joyce Industry: A Reassessment", YEATS, JOYCE, AND BECKETT: NEW LIGHT ON THREE MODERN IRISH WRITERS, eds Kathleen McGrory and John Unterecker (Lewisburg, Pa.: Bucknell University Press, 1976), pp. 118–32

A lively mid-seventies overview of the current scholarship in Joyce studies. Benstock discusses over eighty books and articles.

A14   Rice, Thomas Jackson
JAMES JOYCE: A GUIDE TO RESEARCH (New York and London: Garland, 1982)

An annotated secondary bibliography which includes "all English and foreign language books, essay collections, monographs, pamphlets, and special periodical issues concerned with Joyce". Articles and chapters on Joyce are chosen more selectively. The entries include careful, accurate annotations (except for foreign works) which evaluate as well as describe contents. Rice's book is distinguished by a clarity of organization and breadth of coverage. In addition, he provides an excellent system of cross-reference which speeds access to information.

A15   Staley, Thomas F.
"James Joyce", RECENT RESEARCH ON ANGLO-IRISH WRITERS: A SUPPLEMENT TO ANGLO-IRISH LITERATURE: A REVIEW OF RESEARCH, ed. Richard J. Finneran (New York: Modern Language Association, 1983), pp. 181–202

A five-year supplement to the first bibliographical essay (in Finneran's ANGLO-IRISH LITERATURE: A REVIEW OF RESEARCH, 1976) presented in the same discursive and critical format.

A16   Feshbach, Sidney, and William Herman
"The History of Joyce Criticism and Scholarship", A COMPANION TO JOYCE STUDIES, eds Jack Bowen and James F. Carens (Westport, Conn., and London: Greenwood Press, 1984), pp. 727–80

Provides a brief history of Joyce criticism including primary and secondary bibliography, biography and letters. A further section on general studies is divided into a selective annotated survey of criticism on Joyce's individual works. The following are not covered: editions of Joyce's work and textual issues, manuscript holdings, and surveys of criticism in a specific historical period.

A17   Hayashi, Tetsumaro, ed.
JAMES JOYCE: RESEARCH OPPORTUNITIES AND DISSERTATION ABSTRACTS (Jefferson, N.C.: McFarland, 1985)

Provides a good information source both for graduate

students seeking new approaches to Joyce for their dissertations and for dissertation directors who need a convenient survey of what has been done already. Includes abstracts from more than 300 dissertations dealing with Joyce in general, his individual works, and comparative studies ranging from the first dissertation on Joyce in 1942 to those recorded up to 1984. An introductory essay by Gary Phillips traces the trends in dissertations on Joyce over the years and offers several suggestions for fresh dissertation topics. This book is also helpful in assisting professional scholars interested in avoiding repetition and locating dissertations on microfilm for research on Joyce and related subjects.

Biographical and Background Studies

Biographical Studies and Memoirs by Contemporaries

Background and Milieu Studies

Biographical information is frequently included in critical studies, just as many of the entries in this section include critical commentary. Works in this section, however, are primarily biographical and are not cross-listed in the critical sections. Frank Budgen's book (B4) is an exception and, although listed in this section because of its biographical importance, is equally valuable for its commentary on *Ulysses*. The distinction between biographical studies and background investigations is frequently a matter of emphasis and a division is made largely for the ease of reference.

See also: G5

Biographical Studies and Memoirs by Contemporaries

B1   Collins, Joseph
      "Ireland's Latest Library Antinomian: James Joyce", THE DOCTOR LOOKS AT LITERATURE (London: Allen and Unwin, 1923), pp. 35–60

      Throughout his life, Joyce had severe health problems, the most formidable of which was eye disease. Collins touches on this latter topic and its effects on Joyce's life.

B2   Anderson, Margaret
      MY THIRTY YEARS WAR (New York: Covici-Friede, 1930)

      Sparse anecdotes of Joyce and his contemporaries, both European and American, recorded by the editor of the *Little Review*, the magazine that published *Ulysses* serially beginning in March 1918. Briefly touches on the public outrage provoked, including the burning of the journal by the US Post Office.

B3   Benco, Silvio
"James Joyce in Trieste", *Bookman* (New York), 72 (1930), 375–80

Benco, an Italian critic and publisher as well as a close friend of Joyce, writes on Joyce's Trieste years. (Reprinted in B37.)

B4   Budgen, Frank
JAMES JOYCE AND THE MAKING OF ULYSSES (London: Grayson, 1934); reissued with additional material as JAMES JOYCE AND THE MAKING OF ULYSSES, AND OTHER WRITINGS, comp. Clive Hart (London: Oxford University Press, 1972)

Called by Hugh Kenner "the best ever written about Joyce". Budgen's book is a sensitive combination of relevant biographical detail and critical commentary that describes the genesis of the novel and reveals a sympathetic awareness of Joyce's art. Budgen illuminates Joyce's conscious craft and the human dimensions of the novel through letters, personal remembrances and perceptive observations of the novel itself. The revised edition includes three new essays that provide further recollections of Joyce as well as critical material.

B5   Magee, William K. (John Eglinton)
"The Beginnings of Joyce" and "A Glimpse of the Later Joyce", IRISH LITERARY PORTRAITS (London: Macmillan, 1935)

Eglinton recounts meetings with Joyce as a young man and a later meeting with Joyce in Paris.

B6   Gogarty, Oliver St John
AS I WAS GOING DOWN SACKVILLE STREET (London: Cowan, 1937), pp. 293–99 and passim

One of the more significant autobiographical writings of Gogarty, who, forever piqued at having been cast as Buck Mulligan, is less respectful than most.

B7   Giedion-Welcker, Carola, ed.
IN MEMORIAM JAMES JOYCE (Zurich: Fretz and Wasmuth, 1941)

Includes a number of essays of biographical importance as well as Professor Heinrich Straumann's burial speech for Joyce.

B8   Soupault, Philippe
SOUVENIRS DE JAMES JOYCE (Algiers, 1943; Paris: Charlot, 1945)

Provides personal background to Joyce's Paris years. Includes fragments from *Finnegans Wake*, of which Soupault was one of the translators.

B9   Edel, Leon
JAMES JOYCE: THE LAST JOURNEY (New York: The Gotham Book Mart, 1947)

A sensitive sketch of Joyce's last days in Zurich.

B10   Léon, Lucie
JAMES JOYCE & PAUL L. LÉON: THE STORY OF A FRIENDSHIP (New York: The Gotham Book Mart, 1948)

Lucie Léon (Lucie Noel) has traced Joyce's twelve-year friendship with her husband, Paul Léon, during Joyce's late years in Paris.

B11   Gormon, Herbert S.
James Joyce (1940); rev. edn, New York: Rinehart, 1948)

This was the only biography available prior to 1959, but it is in no sense definitive, as some have claimed. Although Gorman's work is not to be discounted, it remains a biography written by one loyal to the subject and dependent upon him for access to nearly all material. Gorman had both the advantages and disadvantages of a close relationship with Joyce, and his book clearly reveals this. As Richard Ellmann's unparalleled biography of Joyce indicates, his own access to letters and material, as well as the candour offered by Joyce's friends and relatives after his death, far outweighed Gorman's advantage of having known Joyce personally. In fact, Gorman's relationship with Joyce on occasion was a detriment, for Joyce actively interfered and at least once exercised a veto over material to be included.

B12   Jolas, Maria, ed.
A JAMES JOYCE YEARBOOK (Paris: Transition Press, 1949)

Best known for its inclusion of Hermann Broch's essay on Joyce. Jolas has collected biographical material by several writers and critics who knew Joyce or followed his work from the vantage point of Paris. Included are Stuart Gilbert, Heinrich Straumann and Paul Léon.

B13   Svevo, Italo
JAMES JOYCE: A LECTURE DELIVERED IN MILAN IN 1927, trans. Stanislaus Joyce (New York: New Directions, 1950; San Francisco: City Lights Books, 1950)

Originally published in a limited edition as a Christmas gift. Svevo was a friend of Joyce's in Trieste, and Joyce helped him to achieve recognition as a novelist. His comments on Joyce are interesting and revealing, because Svevo was engaged with many of the same problems of shaping fictional characters, that Joyce had encountered.

B14   Sheehy, Eugene
MAY IT PLEASE THE COURT (Dublin: Fallon, 1951)

A humorous autobiography that recalls Joyce in his university days with Thomas Kettle and Francis Sheehy-Skeffington, with the latter of whom Joyce collaborated in the publication of the *Two Essays* pamphlet, Joyce's first published work, except for the lost *Et Tu Healy*.

B15   Byrne, John Francis
SILENT YEARS: AN AUTOBIOGRAPHY, WITH MEMOIRS OF JAMES JOYCE AND OUR IRELAND (New York: Farrar, Strauss and Young, 1953)

Especially rich in contemporary Dublin background. In 1909 Joyce visited Byrne at No. 7 Eccles Street, an address later immortalized as the Blooms' house in *Ulysses*. More important, Byrne was the model for the character of Cranly in *A Portrait*, and his book recalls many experiences shared with Joyce that found their way into Joyce's books.

B16   Giedion-Welcker, C. (arola)
"*James Joyce in Zurich*", THE GOLDEN HORIZON, ed. Cyril Connolly (New York: University Books, 1955), pp. 383–87

Joyce's good friend Giedion-Welcker provides a sensitive account of Joyce's years in Zurich.

B17   MacDiarmid, Hugh
IN MEMORIAM JAMES JOYCE (Glasgow: MacLellan, 1955)

Although primarily an account of MacDiarmid's own literary development and interest in language, the volume also includes poems by this Scottish poet devoted to Joyce's inspiration and memory. While not strictly biographical, MacDiarmid's poems evoke a spiritual heritage.

B18   Magalaner, Marvin, and Richard M. Kain
"Part I—The Man", JOYCE: THE MAN, THE WORK, THE REPUTATION (New York: New York University Press, 1956), pp. 3–43

Provides two important essays that appeared prior to Ellmann's biography, Kain's "The Joyce Enigma" and Magalaner's "The Problem of Biography". These pieces are quite valuable and succeed in offering points of departure for further investigation. Other aspects of this work are discussed in D12.

B19   Colum, Mary, and Padraic Colum
OUR FRIEND JAMES JOYCE (Garden City, N.Y.: Doubleday, 1958)

The book records Joyce's friendship with Padraic Colum, the

Irish poet, and his wife Mary, a perceptive critic and writer. The Colums knew Joyce throughout most of his life, including his Dublin years at the turn of the century and his later life in Paris. Although largely anecdotal, the book offers a witty portrait of their extended encounters with Joyce.

B20   Gillet, Louis
CLAYBOOK FOR JAMES JOYCE (1941); trans. Georges Markow-Totevy, New York: Abelard-Schuman, 1958)

Provides a good account of Joyce's literary associations and activities in Paris and also the French reaction to and acceptance of his work.

B21   Joyce, Stanislaus
MY BROTHER'S KEEPER: JAMES JOYCE'S EARLY YEARS, ed. with introduction and notes by Richard Ellmann; preface T. S. Eliot (New York: Viking, 1958)

This work offers a thorough, if slightly biased, account of Joyce's early years in Dublin and is especially valuable for the information it provides on Joyce's immediate family background and his early struggles to become a writer. Together with the rich collection of correspondence, this volume forms an excellent record of the close, if frequently strained, relationship between the two brothers.

B22   Beach, Sylvia
SHAKESPEARE AND COMPANY (New York: Harcourt, 1959)

Although a general account of her bookshop, a substantial section is devoted to Joyce and the publication of *Ulysses*. Beach also discusses the complexities and difficulties of being Joyce's publisher and offers an account of his family circumstances.

B23   Ellmann, Richard
JAMES JOYCE (1959; rev. edn, New York and London: Oxford University Press, 1982)

This authoritative biography is considered by many to be the

most important work to be written on Joyce. It not only made
an enormous contribution to Joyce studies but also to modern
literary biography. The work is noted for thoroughness,
general accuracy, method of presentation, insight, sophistication, style and comprehensive understanding of Joyce as
writer and man. So much of what had been tentative,
unestablished or speculative became fixed and certain after
Ellmann's biography. The revised edition is a slightly
retouched version of the original biography. Ellmann has
added data including names, titles and corrections amounting
to several hundred insertions. He also includes new anecdotes
and letters (such as Adrienne Monnier's letter to Joyce on his
mistreatment of Sylvia Beach). The effect of these revisions
should not be overestimated, however, since this edition does
not alter Ellmann's original portrait of Joyce given in the 1959
biography. The main additional strength is an expanded index
offering detailed subtopics to structure main entries, and an
enlarged photo gallery.

B24   Joyce, Stanislaus
       THE DUBLIN DIARY OF STANISLAUS JOYCE, ed.
       George H. Healy (London: Faber and Faber, 1962; Ithaca,
       N.Y.: Cornell University Press, 1962). Revised and published
       as THE COMPLETE DUBLIN DIARY OF STANISLAUS
       JOYCE (Ithaca, N.Y.: Cornell University Press, 1971)

       A loose collection of personal musings about the Joyce family
       and circle of friends, with particular emphasis on Stanislaus'
       admiration and curiosity over his brother. The diary
       commences at the time of their mother's death in 1903 and
       ends with the departure of James for the continent in 1905.
       These jottings were used by Stanislaus in preparing his
       autobiography, but the two works repeat each other very little.
       The revised edition offers thirty-six pages of additional
       manuscript.

B25   Mercanton, Jacques
       "The Hours of James Joyce", trans. Lloyd C. Parks, *Kenyon
       Review*, 24 (1962), 700–30; 25 (1963), 93–118

       Another good memoir of Joyce during his Paris years.
       (Reprinted in B37.)

B26   Joyce, Stanislaus
       THE MEETING OF SVEVO AND JOYCE (Udine, Italy:
       Del Bianco Editore, 1965)

       A later lecture by Stanislaus given in May 1955 in Trieste
       which traces the Joyce–Svevo friendship.

B27   Pound, Ezra
       POUND/JOYCE: THE LETTERS OF EZRA POUND TO
       JAMES JOYCE, WITH POUND'S ESSAYS ON JOYCE,
       ed. Forrest Read (New York: New Directions, 1967)   .

       Gathers together, within the framework of an historical
       narrative, Pound's surviving letters to Joyce and all of his
       essays and articles on Joyce's work. Read's commentary also
       provides various anecdotes that give literary and biographical
       background.

B28   Anderson, Chester G.
       JAMES JOYCE AND HIS WORLD (New York: Viking,
       1968)

       A thorough and precise biographical account of Joyce, based
       on Anderson's conviction that the details of Joyce's life are
       closely related to the substance of his work. Illustrated by
       copious photographs of Joyce, his family and his sur-
       roundings.

B29   Curran, Constantine P.
       JAMES JOYCE REMEMBERED (London and New York:
       Oxford University Press, 1968)

       The best single account by one of Joyce's contemporaries of
       his Dublin years. Curran and Joyce met as fellow students at
       University College and remained friends throughout Joyce's
       life. Of particular interest is the full description of the
       intellectual and cultural background of Dublin and University
       College which forms an interesting contrast with that offered
       in *A Portrait*.

B30   Budgen, Frank
       "Mr. Joyce", MYSELVES WHEN YOUNG (London and

New York: Oxford University Press, 1970), pp. 181–204

The autobiography of Budgen, a painter who became a close friend of Joyce during the early stages of the composition of *Ulysses*. This is a brief but penetrating portrait of Joyce during his Switzerland years.

B31 Lidderdale, Jane, and Mary Nicholson
DEAR MISS WEAVER: HARRIET SHAW WEAVER, 1876–1961 (New York: Viking, 1970), passim

Joyce's long relationship with Harriet Shaw Weaver, his patroness and friend, is covered in this excellent study. Because of Weaver's association with the *Egoist* and her sustained interest in Joyce's career, this is an especially valuable book for, among other things, its account of the publishing of Joyce's work.

B32 Ryan, John, ed.
A BASH IN THE TUNNEL: JAMES JOYCE BY THE IRISH (Brighton, England: Clifton Books, 1970)

Offers a collection of memoirs by Joyce's contemporaries and a younger generation of Irish writers who lived and wrote under Joyce's shadow. These writers tell how they encountered Joyce as a person and as a legend, recording the intellectual and emotional impact upon their own writings. Joyce studies have so often and quite properly focused on Joyce as a continental writer that the Irish background frequently has been submerged, but biographical works such as this one reinforce the importance of Ireland as a shaping and controlling element in Joyce's development as well as his legacy to and influence on his countrymen. Among the contributors are Beckett (a reprint of his contribution to *Our Exagmination* ...), Patrick Kavanagh, Benedict Kiely, and Niall Montgomery.

B33 Rodgers, W. R., ed.
IRISH LITERARY PORTRAITS: W. B. YEATS: JAMES JOYCE: GEORGE MOORE: J. M. SYNGE: GEORGE BERNARD SHAW: OLIVER ST JOHN GOGARTY: F. R. HIGGINS: A. E. (GEORGE RUSSELL) (London: British Broadcasting Corporation, 1972)

Contains edited transcriptions of two BBC interviews with a circle of Joyce's friends. Included in the group commenting both on Joyce as a young man and as a mature artist are: Gogarty, Eva and Stanislaus Joyce, Carola Giedion-Welcker, Maria Jolas, Harriet Weaver, Sylvia Beach, Adrienne Monnier and Frank Budgen.

B34   Power, Arthur
CONVERSATIONS WITH JAMES JOYCE, ed. Clive Hart (New York: Barnes and Noble, 1974)

Records the friendship between Joyce and the Irish artist-expatriate Power during the 1920s in Paris. Joyce is portrayed as speaking unguardedly about such writers as Hardy, Ibsen, Proust, Synge, and also about his own works. Reveals a personable side of Joyce that counteracts his image as a reticent, remote genius.

B35   Davies, Stan Gebler
JAMES JOYCE: A PORTRAIT OF THE ARTIST (London: Davis-Poynter, 1975)

An insignificant work marked by its mean-spirited comments on the man and some humorous commentary on the Dublin literary scene. Davies follows either Ellmann or Ellmann's sources, and when he veers away from Ellmann, as he does only occasionally, he makes errors.

B36   McMillan, Dougald
TRANSITION: THE HISTORY OF A LITERARY ERA, 1927–1938 (New York: Braziller, 1976), pp. 179–231 and passim

Includes a good account of Joyce's relationship to Jolas and *transition*, the literary journal that published sections of *Finnegans Wake* as "Work in Progress".

B37   Potts, Willard, ed.
PORTRAITS OF THE ARTIST IN EXILE: RECOLLECTIONS OF JAMES JOYCE BY EUROPEANS (Seattle: University of Washington Press, 1979; New York: Harcourt Brace, 1986)

An excellent collection of memoirs on Joyce by European friends and acquaintances. Represented are Silvio Benco, Alessandro Francini-Bruni, August Suter, Nino Frank, Carola Giedion-Welcker, Jacques Mercanton and others. Francini-Bruni recalls Joyce as a fellow Berlitz teacher in Zurich and Giedion-Welcker describes her involvement with the Joyce family in Zurich. Seven of the reminiscences appear for the first time in English. This is a well-edited collection with informative headnotes, substantial identifications in the footnotes and accurate translations from the various European languages.

B38   O'Brien, Edna
"Joyce & Nora: A Portrait of Joyce's Marriage", *Harper's*, 261 (September 1980): also published as PORTRAIT (Northridge, Calif.: Lord John Press, 1981)

A biographical meditation on the Joyces' relationship that combines a breezy entertaining style with fact, textual quotes, and a good deal of speculation. This is not a work of biographical scholarship but an impressionistic narrative of the trials and tribulations of the Joyce romance from the point of view of a later Irish novelist.

B39   Costello, Peter
JAMES JOYCE (Dublin: Gill and Macmillan, 1980)

A brief biographical introduction.

B40   Frank, Katherine
"Writing Lives: Theory and Practice in Literary Biography", *Genre*, 13:4 (Winter 1980), 499–516

A comparison of Ellmann's biography of Joyce with Leon Edel's biography of Henry James. An interesting essay that opens up several avenues of speculation with regard to writing about an author's life.

B41   Bradley, Bruce, S. J.
JAMES JOYCE'S SCHOOLDAYS (Dublin: Gill and Macmillan, 1982; New York: St Martin's, 1982)

The most complete study available on young Joyce's academic career at Clongowes Wood and Belvedere Colleges. It presents recently discovered school documents, photos and biographical details which clarify Joyce's actual experiences at those schools. Bradley draws extensive parallels between his documentary evidence and *A Portrait's* stylised account. The author, a master at Belvedere, also provides insight into the Jesuit educational system, a major influence on Joyce's mind and art.

B42   O'Laoi, Padraic
        NORA BARNACLE JOYCE (Galway: Kenny Bookshop and Art Galleries, 1982)

A biographical study of Nora Barnacle, including her early life in Galway, her residence in Dublin and eventual elopement with Joyce. The reading of Nora's character is a sympathetic one, stressing her loyalty, courage, and humour in the face of a difficult relationship. This view is perhaps biased, even rose-coloured, but helps to balance the impression that Nora was inadequate to sustain Joyce in his endeavours.

B43   Fitch, Noel Riley
        SYLVIA BEACH AND THE LOST GENERATION: LITERARY PARIS IN THE TWENTIES AND THIRTIES (New York: W. W. Norton and Co., 1983)

Depicts the Paris literary scene of the 1920s and 1930s as centred around Sylvia Beach and her bookstore, Shakespeare and Company. Of particular interest to students of Joyce are Fitch's interpretations of the Joyce/Beach relationship, which occupy a major portion of the book. Her interpretations, however, are not based on literary analysis or judgement, but are a biographical act examining literary and personal relationships in the light of documentary evidence and some, perhaps casual, speculation.

B44   Staley, Thomas F.
        "James Joyce and One of His Ghosts: Edouard Dujardin", *Renascence*, 35:2 (Winter 1983), 85–95

Traces Joyce's long-standing interest in the French writer, Wagnerite, and Symbolist, whose novel, *Les Lauriers sont coupés*, was claimed by Joyce to have been his prototype for stream-of-consciousness narration. This essay produces letters for the first time that document Joyce's close interest in promoting Dujardin's career as a writer.

Background and Milieu Studies

B45   Hutchins, Patricia
JAMES JOYCE'S DUBLIN (London: Grey Walls Press, 1950)

An illustrated volume that emphasizes Joycean locales in Dublin. Included are accounts of houses in which Joyce lived, statues he passed, seascapes, buildings, and parks he strolled by. The Dublin photographed in this volume is no longer there today.

B46   Hutchins, Patricia
JAMES JOYCE'S WORLD (London: Methuen, 1957)

Offers a general topographical background to Joyce. This book has been superseded by Ellmann's biography and later works, but it provides a good general literary and biographical background in its emphasis on geographical location and literary activity contemporaneous with Joyce's writing.

B47   Howarth, Herbert
"James Augustine Joyce, 1882–1941", THE IRISH WRITERS, 1880–1940: LITERATURE UNDER PARNELL'S STAR (London: Rockliff, 1958), pp. 243–87

This is an excellent chapter on Joyce's work in relation to political life, Irish nationalism, and the mythic elements that developed in Anglo-Irish literature after Parnell's fall.

B48   Sullivan, Kevin
JOYCE AMONG THE JESUITS (New York: Columbia University Press, 1958)

A meticulous account of Joyce's academic career emphasizing the influence of the Catholic heritage on his work. Sullivan makes extremely close comparison of factual and primary materials, such as class records, grade reports, school catalogues, contemporary sketches of faculty members with whom Joyce came into contact, retreat manuals, text books, and student themes. This study helped shift critical opinion away from the loose biographical assumptions made about Joyce, which were derived from *A Portrait* and *Stephen Hero.* Sullivan demonstrates the essential separation between Joyce and his character Stephen Dedalus.

B49   Morse, J. Mitchell
THE SYMPATHETIC ALIEN: JAMES JOYCE AND CATHOLICISM (New York: New York University Press, 1959)

An intellectual-historical account of Joyce's artistic confrontation with the church fathers, such as Scotus, Aquinas, William of Occam and Ignatius Loyola. The general tone as well as certain theses produced some sharp replies, especially from dissenting Jesuits. Overall, the view Morse presents of the Jesuits is harsh and unconvincing.

B50   Tindall, William York
THE JOYCE COUNTRY (1960; rev. edn, New York: Schocken, 1972)

An excellent collection of Dublin photographs related to Joyce's works. Includes eighty-three pictures, each accompanied by a corresponding passage from Joyce's work. As more of Joyce's Dublin is razed each year, volumes such as Tindall's become increasingly valuable for student and scholar alike.

B51   Kain, Richard M.
DUBLIN IN THE AGE OF WILLIAM BUTLER YEATS AND JAMES JOYCE (Norman: University of Oklahoma Press, 1962)

A most valuable background study of Joyce's contemporary Dublin. This book provides important chapters on the political and cultural ambience of Dublin as well as Joyce's relationship to the writers of the Irish Revival. Kain's book is more than an introduction to the subject, but as an introduction, it is superb.

B52   Pinguentini, Gianni
JAMES JOYCE IN ITALIA (Florence: Libreria Commissionaria Sansoni, 1963)

An idiosyncratic and anecdotal work that recounts interesting biographical incidents of Joyce's life in Trieste and makes intriguing, if far-fetched, speculations regarding Joyce's links with Italian futurism and his contact with other literary and cultural movements to which he was in one way or another exposed during his Trieste years.

B53   Freund, Gisele, and V. B. Carleton
JAMES JOYCE IN PARIS: HIS FINAL YEARS (New York: Harcourt, 1965)

A volume of handsome photographs that document Joyce's later days in Paris, 1938–39. Included are candid shots of Joyce working or with friends and family. Especially noteworthy are photos of Joyce and his grandson, Stephen Joyce.

B54   Crise, Stelio
EPIPHANIES AND PHADOGRAPHS: JOYCE E TRIESTE, (Milan: All'insegna del pesce d'oro, 1967)

An interesting and curious work which tries to recreate Joyce's experience in Trieste through a biographical narrative, partially seen as if through Joyce's consciousness.

B55   Ellmann, Richard
JAMES JOYCE'S TOWER (Dun Laoghaire: Eastern Regional Tourism Organization, 1969)

An attractive twenty-four page volume which includes many of the legal papers related to the Martello tower as well as photographs and appropriate letters associated with Joyce's stay there.

B56   Pearl, Cyril
DUBLIN IN BLOOMTIME: THE CITY JAMES JOYCE KNEW (New York: Viking, 1969)

In spite of several blatant errors, this book provides, in addition to turn-of-the-century photographs, a kind of popular culture background of Dublin during Joyce's early years. It reproduces newspaper headlines, advertisements, want ads, cartoons, and musical programmes in an attempt to capture the everyday life of Dublin during this period. Pearl's text is informative, if not exact, on this background.

B57   Henchy, Deirdre
        "Dublin 80 Years Ago", *Dublin Historical Record,* 26 (1972), 18–35

        A fine essay in social history which describes life in Dublin in Joyce's day. Well documented and informative, it gives careful attention to the economic and civic aspects of the city.

B58   Lyons, John B.
        JAMES JOYCE AND MEDICINE (Dublin: Dolmen, 1973)

        The most thorough study of Joyce's medical and psychological history. The study also attempts to show the effects of Joyce's illnesses on his work. This book, however, is more notable for its medical than its literary speculations.

B59   Cianci, Giovanni
        LA FORTUNA DI JOYCE IN ITALIA: SAGGIO E BIBLIOGRAFIA (1917–72) (Bari, Italy: Adriatica, 1974)

        A thorough study of Joyce's reputation in Italy. This work is noted here because it provides a complete chronological bibliography of Joyce's work published in Italian and also criticism published on Joyce in Italy.

B60   Daly, Leo
        JAMES JOYCE AND THE MULLINGAR CONNECTION (Republic of Ireland: Dolmen [1975]; Atlantic Highlands, N.J.: Humanities Press, 1975)

        A monograph on Joyce's connections with the Irish town of Mullingar with references to its use in his work.

B61   Quinn, Edward
        JAMES JOYCE'S DUBLIN, WITH THE SELECTED
        WRITING FROM JOYCE'S WORKS (London: Secker and
        Warburg, 1975)

        Photographic work on Joyce which is interspersed with
        excerpts from the canon.

Source Materials

This section includes manuscript and pre-publication materials, catalogues and holdings in university libraries, and descriptions of Joyce's own library.

See also: D62, D74, G5, J22 and J6.

C1   Cohn, Alan
      JAMES JOYCE: AN EXHIBITION FROM THE COLLEC-
      TION OF DR H. K. CROESSMANN (Carbondale: Southern
      Illinois University, 1957)

      Brief and selective description of the strong Joyce collection at
      Southern Illinois University.

C2   Thornton, Weldon
      "Books and Manuscripts by James Joyce", *Library Chronicle
      of the University of Texas* (Austin: The University of Texas
      Press, 1961)

      Description of Joyce materials at the University of Texas,
      which has rich holdings in primary materials as well as great
      strength in materials related to modern literature generally.
      Subsequent to the publication of this description, the
      Humanities Research Center at the University of Texas
      acquired Joyce's Trieste library. (See C10.)

C3   Scholes, Robert
      THE CORNELL JOYCE COLLECTION: A CATALOGUE
      (Ithaca, N.Y.: Cornell University Press, 1961)

      The Cornell holdings are strong in materials related to Joyce's
      life and work prior to 1920. The Cornell Collection consists
      largely of the private papers that were in the possession of
      Joyce's brother, Stanislaus.

C4   Spielberg, Peter
      JAMES JOYCE MANUSCRIPTS AND LETTERS AT

THE UNIVERSITY OF BUFFALO: A CATALOGUE
(Buffalo, N.Y.: University of Buffalo Press, 1962)

The Buffalo Collection contains nearly 450 items, 20,000 written pages. A major portion of this collection consists of manuscripts, letters and books acquired in 1950 from Sylvia Beach.

C5 Groden, Michael, gen. ed.
THE JAMES JOYCE ARCHIVE, 63 vols (New York: Garland, 1977–80)

To describe the magnitude of this work properly would require extended commentary. The *Archive,* printed on acid-free paper, publishes in available facsimile all extant and available notes, drafts, manuscripts, typescripts and proofs—Joyce's entire "workshop". Letters are not included. Each *Archive* volume contains a preface by one of the editors, and collectively the *Archive* reproduces some 2,500 pages of original documents from all of the known Joyce collections. This work brings together in one place the widely and erratically dispersed pre-publication materials, but as Michael Groden, one of the chief editors, cautions in his general introduction to the *Archive* index: "It must be recognized ... that these volumes are only reproductions, and a scholar would be irresponsible to rely exclusively on them." The *Archive* is a cornerstone research tool in Joyce studies. One minor disappointment is that each volume is not numbered on the spine or elsewhere.

C6 Connolly, Thomas E. and K. C. Gay, comps
JAMES JOYCE: A DESCRIPTIVE CATALOGUE OF AN EXHIBITION OF MANUSCRIPTS, NOTEBOOKS, TYPE-SCRIPTS, PAGE PROOFS, ETC. IN THE LOCKWOOD MEMORIAL LIBRARY, STATE UNIVERSITY OF NEW YORK AT BUFFALO (Buffalo: Lockwood Library, State University of New York, 1978)

This catalogue contains only a representative portion of the Buffalo holdings, but its chronological arrangement gives it solidity. Items included range from the early epiphanies to the page proofs of *Finnegans Wake* bound in a dust jacket that Faber and Faber sent to Joyce for his birthday in 1939.

C7   Groden, Michael, ed.
        JAMES JOYCE'S MANUSCRIPTS: AN INDEX TO THE
        JAMES JOYCE ARCHIVE (New York: Garland, 1980)

A comprehensive index to the sixty-three volume work *The
James Joyce Archive,* the indispensable reproduction of
Joyce's manuscripts. Groden's index gives the most complete
checklist of all extant manuscripts, typescripts and proofs, and
also includes an index to the various library collections that
hold Joyce manuscript material.

C8   Kemnitz, Charles, comp.
        JAMES JOYCE AT 101: AN EXHIBITION, Exhibition
        Catalogue (Tulsa, Okla.: McFarlin Library, The University of
        Tulsa, 1983)

A brochure that describes the Joyce collections at The
University of Tulsa. The books and manuscripts selected
reflect Joyce's major publications and range from unpublished
letters and first editions to manuscripts of his critical reviews
and major critical texts. The majority of books come from the
Harriet Shaw Weaver collection which contains an unusually
complete record of Joyce's publications, reflecting his
relationship with both *The Egoist* and Shakespeare and
Company presses. What gaps did exist in the Weaver
Collection are filled by materials from other University of
Tulsa collections, notably Cyril Connolly's library and
Edmund Wilson's library. Subsequent to the publication of
this catalogue, the University of Tulsa acquired the papers of
Richard Ellmann which include all his files from the
preparation of his Joyce biography.

C9   THE PAUL AND LUCIE LÉON/JAMES JOYCE
        COLLECTION (Tulsa, Okla.: McFarlin Library, The
        University of Tulsa, 1983)

A catalogue which lists materials from the personal library of
Paul Léon, a close friend and confidant of Joyce. The
catalogue is organised to reflect the collection's development:
works by Joyce and items associated with his work with Paul
Léon, Lucie (Léon) Noel's writings and correspondence, and
miscellaneous pieces collected by Lucie Léon.

C10　Gillespie, Michael Patrick
　　　JAMES JOYCE'S TRIESTE LIBRARY: A CATALOGUE
　　　OF MATERIALS AT THE HARRY RANSOM
　　　HUMANITIES RESEARCH CENTER THE
　　　UNIVERSITY OF TEXAS AT AUSTIN (Austin, Texas: The
　　　University of Texas at Austin, 1986)

　　　An index to the personal library of Joyce during the Trieste
　　　period between 1904 and 1920. This library, reconstructed on
　　　the authority of Richard Ellmann, purportedly records the
　　　reading interests and influences on Joyce during the
　　　intermediary stages of his creative process. Gillespie provides
　　　detailed remarks on marginalia (usually pencil marks) and
　　　relates the significance of individual books to Joyce's work.
　　　The controversy continues over the importance of this library:
　　　whether ownership of a library constitutes a system of
　　　influence, the fact that Joyce chose to leave these books
　　　behind in Trieste, and the accuracy and completeness of
　　　reconstruction of a library that had become dispersed in the
　　　years following Joyce's death. Nevertheless this is a detailed
　　　and useful study for the intellectual sources behind Joyce's
　　　writing.

General and Comparative Studies

General Books
Articles & Chapters in Books
Special Issues

The works in this section treat in various degrees Joyce's entire canon. Where appropriate they are cross-listed in the sections covering Joyce's specific works. Although some entries might seem to focus on only one work, they are annotated in this section because they are broader than the title indicates (D108) or the subject has important implications for Joyce's work generally (D109). Subsection 3 lists commemorative volumes and special issues of journals that are entirely or primarily devoted to Joyce. In cases where special issues treat exclusively one of Joyce's works, such as the frequent special issues of the *James Joyce Quarterly*, they are included in the appropriate individual work sections (in the books subsection).

General Books

D1   Duff, Charles
        JAMES JOYCE AND THE PLAIN READER: AN ESSAY
        (London: Harmsworth, 1932)

        Of little value other than assessing the symptoms of the very limited and mundane critical understanding of Joyce at this time in England, ten years after the publication of *Ulysses.*

D2   Golding, Louis
        JAMES JOYCE (London: Butterworth, 1933)

        A study that suffers from the misconceptions prevailing in the earlier studies of Joyce which reflect the failure of critics to absorb the innovation of Joyce's work.

D3   Martin, Violet F. (Martin Ross)

MUSIC AND JAMES JOYCE (Chicago: Argus Book Shop, 1936)

An exploratory work that studies the influence of Joyce's musical background on his writing, especially in "Work in Progress" (*Finnegans Wake*).

D4   Levin, Harry
JAMES JOYCE: A CRITICAL INTRODUCTION (1941; 2nd edn, New York: New Directions, 1960)

The first thorough and critically astute general book-length study. After forty years of subsequent Joyce scholarship, it still remains a largely reliable study filled with intelligent understanding and sound critical judgement. Levin's book widened Joyce's appeal among sophisticated readers and helped make Joyce "respectable" within the academic community. His book also placed Joyce in the tradition of modern European literature and viewed him as a major figure in this tradition. Wisely, the augmented and revised edition adds a chapter entitled "Revisiting Joyce", but does not alter the prescient insights of the original.

D5   Wilder, Thornton
JAMES JOYCE, 1882–1941 (Aurora, N.Y.: Wells College Press, 1944)

A brief obituary by a writer who admired Joyce throughout his own career and spent much of his life studying *Finnegans Wake*. In this piece he concentrates on Joyce's "comic genius". Wilder was among the first handful of American critics to appreciate Joyce's genius.

D6   Givens, Seon, ed.
JAMES JOYCE: TWO DECADES OF CRITICISM (1948; rev. edn, New York: Vanguard Press, 1963)

An important collection of essays which brought together many of the major early writings on Joyce and gave focus to Joyce's increasingly higher stature in modern literature. Included are essays by a number of Joyce's friends (Budgen, Eugene Jolas and Stuart Gilbert) and Eliot's seminal essay "*Ulysses*, Order and Myth". Among the Americans who contributed to the book and who were later to become important critics of their own generation were Hugh Kenner, S. Foster Damon, William Troy, Joseph Campbell and Frederick J. Hoffman. This collection marked the emergence of the great American interest in Joyce and, in retrospect, it can be seen to signal the American domination of Joyce studies for a number of years.

D7   Strong, Leonard A. G.
THE SACRED RIVER: AN APPROACH TO JAMES JOYCE (London: Methuen, 1949)

A general, introductory work which attempts to present Joyce to a wider audience.

D8   Tindall, William York
JAMES JOYCE: HIS WAY OF INTERPRETING THE MODERN WORLD (New York: Scribner's, 1950)

This study examines the concept of epiphany as a literary technique in Joyce's work. In contrast to previous studies, Tindall's analysis concentrates heavily on the symbolic elements.

D9   Jones, William Powell
JAMES JOYCE AND THE COMMON READER (Norman: University of Oklahoma Press, 1955)

An introductory study that covers Joyce's major canon.

D10   Kenner, Hugh
DUBLIN'S JOYCE (London: Chatto and Windus, 1955; Bloomington: Indiana University Press, 1956).

This book became a springboard from which several controversies arose; these were debated extensively but not conclusively. Kenner begins by discussing Joyce's use of parody and its thematic effects. From this basis he establishes a thesis that the "controlling ideas" in Joyce's work are developed from his analogical vision which emanates from an essentially ironic conception. Thus the fictional world of *Ulysses* (this also applies to *Dubliners* and *A Portrait*), for example, suffused with Joyce's irony, does not directly reveal the author's spriutal values.

Rather, those values lie outside the work, drawn by the ironic implications in the work itself. The detached artist reveals the nature of his antipathy through technique, a technique that forces interpretation outside of the world of the novel. Little that has been subsequently written fails to take into account some aspect of Kenner's arguments. Kenner's powerful insights in this and subsequent works have contributed enormously to Joyce studies and his influence remains singular.

D11   Smidt, Kristian
JAMES JOYCE AND THE CULTIC USE OF
FICTION(1955; rev. edn, New York: Humanities Press, 1959)

A biographical interpretation of Joyce's work, which concludes that Joyce's books are informed by important elements of public ritual and private cult and that these two aspects bring about a "sacral" attachment to Dublin that no amount of ridicule on Joyce's part can obscure. Smidt's work, a rigidly conceived and narrow academic study, takes little risk and offers limited insight.

D12   Magalaner, Marvin, and Richard M. Kain
JOYCE: THE MAN, THE WORK, THE REPUTATION
(New York: New York University Press, 1956)

The first extended treatment of Joyce's critical reputation, the study provides a systematic survey of important aspects of Joyce's life and art, including a thorough appraisal of Joyce's position in modern literature. The authors also stress the many facets of Joyce's personality (Dubliner, Catholic, cynic, among others) as revealed through his work. The Magalaner and Kain volume represented the culmination of Joyce studies through the mid-fifties, and it also pointed to directions that Joyce scholarship should and did take. The volume not only gives an excellent synthesis and evaluation of Joyce studies but also makes its own distinct contribution to the field.

D13   Chatterjee, Sisir
JAMES JOYCE: A STUDY IN TECHNIQUE (1957; 2nd edn, Calcutta: Orient Longmans, 1970)
An amateurish, enthusiastic study of Joyce's fictional technique, is highly derivative and yet ill-informed.

D14   Magalaner, Marvin
        A JAMES JOYCE MISCELLANY (New York: James Joyce
        Society, 1957)

This initial volume in the three-part series (Second Series,
1959; Third Series, 1962) features essays by Thornton Wilder,
Maria Jolas, and Leon Edel. With the exception of Julian
Kaye's essay, which treats the continually perplexing problem
of Joyce's attitude toward the Catholic Church, the essays are
general, appreciative or biographical.

D15   Noon, William T., S. J.
        JOYCE AND AQUINAS (New Haven, Conn.: Yale
        University Press, 1957)

Devotes considerable attention to Joyce's aesthetic theory
while analyzing the entire framework of Joyce's religious
training and educational background. In isolating the
Thomistic aspects of Joyce's works, Noon finds those elements
frequently distorted by Joyce for his own artistic purposes and
theoretical formulations. This point qualifies some rather easy
assumptions from other critics that related Joyce's theories
directly to Aquinas, although Noon does insist, at certain
points perhaps too strongly, upon Joyce's debt to Aquinas. Of
considerable importance in this study are the careful
considerations of the Trinitarian theme in *Ulysses* and its
relation to the Sabellian heresy. Underlying Noon's excellent
study is his inquiry into the vast resourcefulness Joyce
possessed as he transmuted divergent theories, both philosophical and theological, and organized them by way of theme or
image into the structure of his own work.

D16   Stewart, J. I. M.
        JAMES JOYCE (London: Longmans, 1957)

This National Book League pamphlet perhaps succeeds,
despite oversimplification, in its author's purpose of
interpreting Joyce for the general reader. The pamphlet is the
basis for Stewart's longer account of Joyce in *Eight Modern
Writers* (1963) (D131).

D17   Hodgart, Matthew J. C., and Mabel P. Worthington
        SONG IN THE WORK OF JAMES JOYCE (New York:
        Columbia University Press, 1959)

An excellent starting point for the study of the musical aspect of Joyce's work. The authors have traced the song references and noted the sources in Joyce's work and have also included an essay on the function of songs in *Finnegans Wake*.

D18   Magalaner, Marvin
A JAMES JOYCE MISCELLANY, SECOND SERIES
(Carbondale: Southern Illinois University Press, 1959)

This second volume of the three-part series reflects the increasingly scholarly drift in Joyce criticism that began in the fifties. The general quality of the essays is high; most of them take up narrow and specialized interpretive problems or source investigations.

D19   Magalaner, Marvin
TIME OF APPRENTICESHIP: THE FICTION OF
YOUNG JAMES JOYCE (New York: Abelard-Schuman,
1959)

Devotes most attention to *Dubliners* but is also a valuable study of Joyce's growing craftsmanship, of the painstaking care he took to achieve desired effects, and of how he assimilated influences from his reading and allowed them to shape his imagination.

D20   Tindall, William York
A READER'S GUIDE TO JAMES JOYCE (New York:
Noonday, 1959)

This study examines the concept of epiphany as a literary technique in Joyce's work. Tindall places heavy emphasis on the symbolic elements, often to the exclusion of more important narrative and thematic concerns. His study, however, reflects the close readings, explications, and narrow interpretations that dominated Joyce criticism in the fifties.

D21   Goldberg, S. L.
JAMES JOYCE (Edinburgh: Oliver and Boyd, 1962; New
York: Grove Press, 1962)

A sound introduction, though with one qualification. Goldberg dismisses *Finnegans Wake* in a brief final chapter and peevishly rejects all criticism on the work as "a happy hunting-ground for what passes as 'scholarship' and 'research'". Goldberg's case against *Finnegans Wake* can be sympathetically heard, but his contentiousness does not strengthen his points.

D22   Kenner, Hugh
THE STOIC COMEDIANS: FLAUBERT, JOYCE AND BECKETT (Boston: Beacon Press, 1962)

A unique approach which treats the subtleties of Joyce's "comic" verbal techniques and shows how these writers employ "the language of the printed word".

D23   Magalaner, Marvin
A JAMES JOYCE MISCELLANY, THIRD SERIES (Carbondale: Southern Illinois University Press, 1962)

The third of the three-part series provides essays on biographical, critical and historical issues. Magalaner's introduction offers a brief but solid overview of Joyce criticism as it had developed through 1962. The volume reflects interest in manuscript studies, including an unpublished fragment of a story Joyce intended for *Dubliners*, and speculations on the formation of Molly's character through manuscript revisions. There is also a study of Irish allusions and a biographical essay on the parallel between Joyce's personal life and the theme of *Ulysses*.

D24   Ryf, Robert S.
A NEW APPROACH TO JOYCE: THE PORTRAIT OF THE ARTIST AS A GUIDEBOOK (Berkeley and Los Angeles: University of California Press, 1962)

Ryf sees the themes and techniques of the novel as embodying, in their expanded forms, all of Joyce's work. His theory that Joyce uses Stephen's aesthetic theories in his later work has, of course, been largely and correctly discounted. However, Ryf's observations on certain cinematic techniques employed in *A Portrait* are revealing. His study of *A Portrait* attempted to correct or, better, redirect certain critical assumptions which had minimized the work, but his claims are far too strong and ignore the growing aesthetic subtleties and larger dimensions of the later work.

D25   Semmler, Clement
        FOR THE UNCANNY MAN: ESSAYS, MAINLY
        LITERARY (London: Angus and Robertson, 1963; Sydney:
        F. W. Chesire, 1966)

        Largely devoted to general essays on Joyce, but his "James
        Joyce in Australia" is an especially interesting discussion of
        Joyce's reception there—not dissimilar to the initial censorship
        problems in other English-speaking countries. This book is
        not noteworthy as a contribution to Joyce scholarship, but
        suggests the wider range of interest in Joyce that developed
        through the sixties.

D26   Prescott, Joseph
        EXPLORING JAMES JOYCE (Carbondale: Southern
        Illinois University Press, 1964)

        An important collection of essays, most of them previously
        published and widely translated. Of the seven essays, five focus
        on *Ulysses* and one on *Stephen Hero,* and the remaining essay
        is concerned with Joyce's "word technique" throughout his
        canon. Prescott's work, noted for its precision and care,
        represents some of the best early scholarship on Joyce. His
        essays, which address fundamental issues such as the
        characterizations of Stephen Dedalus and Molly Bloom, have
        been used as a starting point by later critics who have dealt
        with these questions. His essay on *Stephen Hero* remains a
        sound introduction to that work today.

D27   Burgess, Anthony
        RE JOYCE (New York: Norton, 1965); published as HERE
        COMES EVERYBODY: AN INTRODUCTION TO
        JAMES JOYCE FOR THE ORDINARY READER
        (London: Faber and Faber, 1965)

        An idiosyncratic work that takes many critical shortcuts and
        makes far too many generalizations. The work often reflects a
        narrow, parochial view of Joyce. Much of what Burgess writes
        has been written more thoroughly before him, but it goes
        unacknowledged. Most interesting are his observations on
        Joyce's use of language—a subject that he understands very
        well.

D28   Adams, Robert M.
        JAMES JOYCE: COMMON SENSE AND BEYOND (New

York: Random House, 1966)

A general study of Joyce's life and work providing a good chapter on the Irish background and its influence on Joyce. Adams is especially interesting in his comments concerning a number of critical issues widely argued earlier by other Joyce critics, including himself (*Surface and Symbol*, 1962). Adams, for example, debunks much of the importance attributed to the epiphany by critics, especially the more sustained arguments that attach central significance to it in Joyce's aesthetic. The last chapter of the book is a brief but convincing essay on the importance of *Finnegans Wake*, and, in the long run, of its larger contribution to modern literature. Adam's book offers a balanced interpretation of Joyce's life and work, a "common sense" approach. Beyond this, however, are occasions when Adams ventures to assail certain critical interpretations or arguments and offer his own often controversial extrapolations.

D29   Cronin, Anthony
A QUESTION OF MODERNITY (London: Secker and Warburg, 1966)

A book of essays largely taken up with defining modernism and exploring the distinctive contribution of the "moderns" with emphasis on Joyce and Beckett.

D30   Goldman, Arnold
THE JOYCE PARADOX: FORM AND FREEDOM IN HIS FICTION (London: Routledge and Kegan Paul, 1966; Evanston, Ill.: Northwestern University Press, 1966)

A study which follows a group of related themes through Joyce's fiction up to *Finnegans Wake*. In the last analysis, Goldman observes, the major issues in Joyce criticism are "questions of the mode of existence of 'symbols' in the fiction and of the quality of Joyce's feeling, the extent of his human sympathies". Goldman also attempts to reconcile major critical approaches which developed during the sixties when Joyce studies shifted from explication to extended interpretation. He sees the apparent paradoxical positions taken with regard to Joyce's work as reflecting the inherent paradoxes in the work itself, even as early as the first *Dubliners* stories. The work insists that paradox is capable of defining itself. For example, Goldman's analysis of the "symbolist" elements in

Joyce and how critical emphasis on these has led to a less appreciative reading of the character of Stephen Dedalus is especially well executed, and it confronts a real crux in Joyce studies. To sustain his interpretation, Goldman draws useful parallels to Kierkegaard and Freud. In the end, however, perhaps Goldman is too generous regarding his fellow critics for he suggests that the wide critical diversity in *Ulysses* is a projection of thematic conflicts within the work; but his critical argument is finely drawn, and summary statements hardly do it justice.

D31   Litz, A. Walton
       JAMES JOYCE (1966, rev. edn, New York: Twayne, 1972)

A fresh and complete introduction to Joyce's life and work, taking into account the enormous critical development in Joyce studies throughout the fifties and early sixties. The precision and clarity of this work, together with Litz's uncanny ability to devote illuminating consideration to the complex problems Joyce presents to his readers, gives the book special value to those who are beginning Joyce studies.

D32   Staley, Thomas, F., ed.
       JAMES JOYCE TODAY: ESSAYS ON THE MAJOR
       WORKS (Bloomington: Indiana University Press, 1966)

Commemorates the twenty-fifth anniversary of Joyce's death. There is an essay on each of Joyce's major works and also an important essay on *Chamber Music* by Herbert Howarth. Of special note is William Blissett's essay "James Joyce in the Smithy of His Soul", which traces the persistent Wagnerian influence on Joyce throughout his literary career and especially the embodiment of the Wagnerian elements in Stephen's character. Clive Hart's "*Finnegans Wake* in Perspective" remains one of the best and most helpful essays on the work.

D33   Harmon, Maurice, ed.
       THE CELTIC MASTER: CONTRIBUTIONS TO THE
       FIRST JAMES JOYCE SYMPOSIUM HELD IN
       DUBLIN (1967; Dublin: Dolmen, 1969)

These essays, possibly excepting Norman Silverstein's "Evolution of the Nighttown Setting", are unimportant, but the contributions by two Dubliners, Niall Montgomery and the late Donagh MacDonagh, are not without charm.

D34　Moseley, Virginia
JOYCE AND THE BIBLE (DeKalb: Northern Illinois
University Press, 1967)

Traces the biblical elements throughout Joyce's canon
devoting a chapter to each work, but she insists in her
generalizations on far too great a reliance upon the Bible in his
work.

D35　O'Brien, Darcy
THE CONSCIENCE OF JAMES JOYCE (Princeton:
Princeton University Press, 1967)

Deals with the moral judgements embodied in Joyce's
writings, an area which has undergone considerable debate.
O'Brien focuses on the sexual element of Irish Catholic
morality and the "indelible mark" it left on Joyce's thinking.
More specifically O'Brien contends that Joyce's early
education and family upbringing left him with a moral disgust
for the world and that his early works reflect this bitterness; it
was only later, when he developed a comic view of man, that
his work was able to reconcile this opposition. Thus, out of
Joyce's guilt-ridden, puritanical, Dublin Catholic background
there emerged a comic view of man's folly that overrode but
left essentially unchanged his fundamental moral outlook.
O'Brien's argument that Joyce was not, as so many writers of
the modernist movement were, a moral relativist is a point well
taken, yet it is not without pitfalls, such as when he extends his
argument into character analysis and thus narrows Joyce's
rich and discriminating process of creation.

D36　Goldman, Arnold
JAMES JOYCE (London: Routledge and Kegan Paul, 1968)

A student's basic introduction to Joyce that includes excerpts
from Joyce's works with good analyses.

D37　Kronegger, Maria Elizabeth
JAMES JOYCE AND ASSOCIATED IMAGE MAKERS
(New Haven, Conn.: College and University Press, 1968)

A discussion of Joyce's imagery that insists on its kinship with

Edgar Allan Poe. The thesis traces Joyce's affinity as an image maker with Poe as Poe's theories are adumbrated and protracted by the French Symbolists, a relationship observed by Edmund Wilson (sans Poe) more broadly many years before. The theory as posed by Kronegger seems curiously wrong-headed, especially in the singularity of vision it attributes to Joyce, but there are in her book some interesting comparisons between the aesthetic theories of the Impressionist painters and Joyce's own early concepts of art.

D38   Murillo, L. A.
THE CYCLICAL NIGHT: IRONY IN JAMES JOYCE AND JORGE LUIS BORGES (Cambridge, Mass.: Harvard University Press, 1968)

Treats the ironic dimension in Joyce from *Stephen Hero* through *Finnegans Wake* and compares it with Borges' use of irony.

D39   Tysdahl, Bjorn J.
JOYCE AND IBSEN: A STUDY IN LITERARY INFLUENCE (New York: Humanities Press, 1968)

A valuable study examining and tracing Ibsen's influence from Joyce's youthful enthusiasm through *Finnegans Wake*.

D40   Zyla, Wolodymyr, T., ed.
JAMES JOYCE: HIS PLACE IN WORLD LITERATURE: PROCEEDINGS OF THE COMPARATIVE LITERATURE SYMPOSIUM, II, FEBRUARY 7 AND 8, 1969 (Lubbock: Interdepartmental Committee on Comparative Literature, Texas Technical College, 1969)

Six original papers presented at a comparative literature conference. These have as their general theme Joyce's contributions to literature outside of the English-speaking countries.

D41   Dahl, Liisa
LINGUISTIC FEATURES OF THE STREAM-OF-CONSCIOUSNESS TECHNIQUES OF JAMES JOYCE, VIRGINIA WOOLF AND EUGENE O'NEILL (Turku, Finland: Turun Yliopisto, 1970)

An excellent comparative study of the way language structure contributes to stream-of-consciousness narrative in these authors.

D42   Deming, Robert H., ed.
JAMES JOYCE: THE CRITICAL HERITAGE, 2 vols
(London: Routledge and Kegan Paul, 1970)

These two volumes form a good survey of contemporary reaction to Joyce's work from 1902 to 1941. The purpose is to provide "as complete as possible a spectrum of the contemporary response" to Joyce's work. Although some of the material could have been more adroitly excerpted, the essays offer a thorough picture of Joyce's critical reputation during his lifetime. The collection is especially valuable because it reprints material inaccessible in many libraries, including foreign items in (if not always the best) English translations. Deming also provides in his introduction a brief general survey of the criticisms on individual works.

D43   Gross, John
JAMES JOYCE (New York: Viking Press, 1970)

Assumes a broader literary background and is enjoyed by one who has thoroughly read most of Joyce. Gross makes many wise statements about Joyce's work and literature in general. Its graceful style does not conceal the author's awareness of the more specialized aspects of Joyce scholarship.

D44   Bates, Ronald, and Harry J. Pollock, eds
LITTERS FROM ALOFT: PAPERS DELIVERED AT
THE SECOND CANADIAN JAMES JOYCE SEMINAR,
MCMASTER UNIVERSITY (Tulsa, Okla.: University of
Tulsa Press, 1971)

These essays are all competent. Michael H. Begnal's "Who Speaks When I Dream? Who Dreams When I speak? A Narrational Approach to *Finnegans Wake*" insists that HCE is not alone in his dreaming. This is the freshest essay in the collection. Maurice Beebe's essay is of interest because it offers further development, with special emphasis on Joyce, of his earlier theories related to the characteristics of modernism.

D45   Brandabur, Edward
        A SCRUPULOUS MEANNESS: A STUDY OF JOYCE'S
        EARLY WORK (Urbana: University of Illinois Press, 1971)

        A psychoanalytical perspective which focuses mainly on
        Dubliners and *Exiles* but also offers commentary on *A
        Portrait* and *Ulysses*.

D46   Cross, Richard K.
        FLAUBERT AND JOYCE: THE RITE OF FICTION
        (Princeton, N.J.: Princeton University Press, 1971)

        Thorough examination of Flaubert and Joyce which deals
        principally with *Ulysses*, though it includes chapters on
        Dubliners and *A Portrait* as well.

D47   Kenner, Hugh
        THE POUND ERA (Berkeley and Los Angeles: University
        of California Press, 1971)

        Offers a rich, kaleidoscopic portrait of the modern period,
        which in turn provides insights into Joyce's art. This is an
        indispensable work for gaining background and understand-
        ing of modernism generally.

D48   Cixous, Hélène
        THE EXILE OF JAMES JOYCE (1968); trans. Sally A. J.
        Purcell (New York: David Lewis, 1972)

        A forerunner of many studies that were to follow in the
        seventies and eighties. This work has certain affinities with
        psychological approaches but is conceived very differently.
        Cixous's biographical treatment of Joyce emanates from the
        context of French criticism that has its roots in Lanson and
        Mornet, but more immediately the work of Roland Barthes.
        Despite many interesting incursions on the Joycean landscape,
        Cixous's book is marked by inaccurate and often preposterous
        generalities. Some, however, have found this study fresh and
        challenging, yet the book's very diffusiveness undermines
        Cixous's attempt to descibe the totality of Joyce's art.

D49   Senn, Fritz, ed.
        NEW LIGHT ON JOYCE FROM THE DUBLIN

SYMPOSIUM (Bloomington: Indiana University Press, 1972)

Includes thirteen papers presented at the 1969 symposium. This collection offers a good representation of the shifting scholarly interests being pursued at that time in Joyce studies. Four essays are concerned with textual and stylistic matters, one with Joyce's politics, another with his views on love and sex. Ihab Hassan's contribution is a "scenario" in eight scenes and introduces this critic's increasing interest in Joyce as the fulcrum between modernism and post-modernism. Leslie Fiedler's contribution is based upon his Bloomsday Dinner speech and offers a highly personal and sympathetic account of Leopold Bloom, the modern Jew in Dublin. As a single volume this book lacks focus, but this is more than made up for in the quality of several of the essays.

D50   Aubert, Jacques
       INTRODUCTION À L'ESTHÉTIQUE DE JAMES JOYCE (Paris: Didier, 1973)

The broadest and most sustained study of the development of Joyce's aesthetic. Paying careful attention to Joyce's own critical essays on such writers as James Clarence Mangan, and to key entries from the notebooks, Aubert ably traces its germination and elaboration. He suggests a much wider possibility of European sources than has been previously recognized and argues convincingly that there is a much greater evolution and change in Joyce's theory than has been grasped before.

D51   Burgess, Anthony
       JOYSPRICK: AN INTRODUCTION TO THE LANGUAGE OF JAMES JOYCE (London: Deutsch, 1973)

Devoted almost exclusively to Joyce's use of language, this book is superior to Burgess' earlier work, for in the latter his instincts are more compatible with the subject. *Joysprick* is in no sense, as Burgess admits in his preface, a systematic linguistic study, but rather an inquiry into Joyce's aesthetic disposition of language. His treatment of Joyce's use of dialect and the implication engendered in his use of names is especially interesting.

D52   Vickery, John B.
THE LITERARY IMPACT OF THE GOLDEN BOUGH
(Princeton: Princeton University Press, 1973)

Includes five chapters on Joyce from the early works through
Finnegans Wake. Vickery compiles an impressive number of
correspondences and parallels between *The Golden Bough*
and Joyce's works, especially *Ulysses*, and these parallels add
to our knowledge of Joyce. Vickery's case for Frazer's
influence on Joyce, however, is severely weakened by the fact
that there is no direct evidence that Joyce was acquainted with
any of Frazer's works.

D53   Bowen, Zack
MUSICAL ALLUSIONS IN THE WORKS OF JAMES
JOYCE: EARLY POETRY THROUGH ULYSSES
(Albany: State University of New York Press, 1974)

Similar to the work of Hodgart and Worthington on
Finnegans Wake. Whereas those authors identify and list song
allusions, Bowen's book is an annotation of musical allusions
and a study of Joyce's use of music in terms of style,
characterization, structure and theme.

D54   Chace, William M., ed.
JOYCE: A COLLECTION OF CRITICAL ESSAYS
(Englewood Cliffs, N.J.: Prentice-Hall, 1974)

Good general introduction covering all of Joyce's work. All
essays have been published previously.

D55   Grose, Kenneth
JAMES JOYCE (London: Evans, 1975)

An introductory study designed for the non-scholarly reader
which traces Joyce's artistic development through his major
works, with particular emphasis on *Ulysses*.

D56   Garvin, John
JAMES JOYCE'S DISUNITED KINGDOM AND THE
IRISH DIMENSION (Dublin: Gill and Macmillan, 1976)

Eccentric study contending that *Ulysses* and *Finnegans Wake* are based on Irish history, folklore and legend, and are deeply rooted in Irish culture generally, a probability that has not escaped earlier critics. From this position, however, Garvin makes many curious and sundry observations, some arcane and interesting, others unformulated, random, and remote. Though unsystematic and frequently bizarre in its interpretations, the book is not without value. Garvin knows a great deal about Dublin, especially nineteenth-century bureaucracy, and can capture the milieu in which Joyce spent his youth.

D57   Knuth, A. M. Leo
THE WINK OF THE WORD: A STUDY OF JAMES
JOYCE'S PHATIC COMMUNICATION (Amsterdam:
Rodopi, 1976)

A study of ingenuity and perception dealing with Joyce's phatic communication. The opening chapters present a close argument for linking Joyce the man and artist to his work; Knuth concentrates on the formation of Joyce's thought and argues against the restrictive and narrow model set up for reading Joyce by S. L. Goldberg in *The Classical Temper* (1961). Knuth's later chapters trace Joyce's movement from realist to multivalent writer, offering a rigorous analysis of passages and sections, such as the treatment of "Wandering Rocks". The book is difficult to summarize, and several of Knuth's larger contentions are elusive; but his commentary on motifs, words and even letter arrangements is engrossing, and his analysis of Shem's riddle in *Finnegans Wake* is highly original.

D58   McGrory, Kathleen, and John Unterecker, eds
YEATS, JOYCE AND BECKETT: NEW LIGHT ON
THREE MODERN IRISH WRITERS (Lewisburg, Pa.:
Bucknell University Press, 1976)

This book, dedicated to William York Tindall, has four essays on Joyce and includes a selection of Tindall's fine photographs of the Joyce landscape. The essay by Raymond J. Porter on Joyce's Irishness and those by Margaret Solomon and Nathan Halper are all strong. Bernard Benstock's essay is a thorough, informative, and often witty discussion of "the Joyce industry". There is also a valuable interview with Joyce's close friend from Zurich, Carola Giedion-Welker.

D59   Mitchell, Breon
JAMES JOYCE AND THE GERMAN NOVEL 1922–1933
(Athens: Ohio University Press, 1976)

Originally a distinguished Oxford dissertation on Joyce's influence on the German novel, Mitchell's volume is a careful and judicious comparative study that deals with Joyce's impact on the development of the German novel in the twenties and thirties.

D60   Adams, Robert M.
AFTERJOYCE: STUDIES IN FICTION AFTER
ULYSSES (New York: Oxford University Press, 1977)

Explores the premise that Joyce, and specifically *Ulysses,* is the major system of influence on twentieth-century writers. Adam treats the influence of stream-of-consciousness techniques on Faulkner and Woolf, Beckett's minimalist reaction to Joyce's style, and Nabokov's acquisition of Joyce's verbal machinery. Adams concludes that only Kafka represents a comparable influence to Joyce on the modern novel, and along much different lines. Dismissing the idea that any historical epoch can be equated with a man's name, Adams suggests that we may still entertain the possibility of "the Joyce Era".

D61   Benstock, Bernard
JAMES JOYCE: THE UNDISCOVER'D COUNTRY (New York: Barnes and Noble, 1977)

Thorough and reliable study of the intricate and complex political and social history that forms so much of the background of Joyce's work. Joyce used Ireland in nearly every way a writer can use his native country, and his fundamental love/hate relation is deeply, and, in a way, hopelessly complex. Benstock holds, and convincingly argues, that ultimately Joyce rejected Ireland and made his commitment to the larger European literary tradition. In arguing his position, Benstock treats the full complex of Irish cultural and political thought that bears so heavily on Joyce's work.

        Ellmann, Richard
D62   THE CONSCIOUSNESS OF JOYCE (London: Faber and Faber, 1977; New York: Oxford University Press, 1977)

In part an outgrowth of his earlier *Ulysses on the Liffey*, this book tries "to measure Joyce's response to his principal sources" and includes a listing of Joyce's Trieste library in 1920. Almost none of the books in this collection is annotated; there are a few markings, but they are not sufficient to suggest any direct response from Joyce to the works that made up his working library during his years in Trieste. Ellmann, obviously at home with *Ulysses,* ponders how Joyce may have interwoven and responded to many of these works, ending the book with a chapter on Joyce and politics. Ellmann's study includes little that is conclusive and lacks the force that marked his earlier work.

D63   Marengo-Vaglio, Carla
       INVITIO ALLA LETTURA DI JAMES JOYCE (Milan: Mursio, 1977)

The best introductory study of Joyce to appear in Italy. This book provides a full chronology of Joyce's life and work, discussions of all the works and a good bibliography.

D64   Peake, C. H.
       JAMES JOYCE: THE CITIZEN AND THE ARTIST (Stanford, Calif.: Stanford University Press, 1977)

An important general and comprehensive study of Joyce's work. Peake's commentaries on *Dubliners* and *A Portrait* are sound and frequently richly suggestive, and his work on *Ulysses* is especially praiseworthy. His sections on the "Nestor", "Proteus", "Aeolus", and "Cyclops" episodes are of particular value for their close and revealing analysis of the texts. In his treatment of "Aeolus" and "Cyclops", Peake's emphasis on the political themes is illuminating, and he is especially informative and original regarding the function of the interpolations in "Cyclops". Peake is a careful reader who knows the previous scholarship very well and does not bore us with half a hundred details that are already known. Peake's study is rare in that it serves both as a fine introduction for the general reader and a valuable book for the specialist as well.

D65   Sorenson, Dolf
       JAMES JOYCE'S AESTHETIC THEORY: ITS DEVELOPMENT AND APPLICATION (Amsterdam: Rodopi, 1977)

A book of limited interest. Sorenson does not even mention in his bibliography Jacques Aubert's important book on the subject, *Introduction à l'esthétique de James Joyce* (Paris, 1973). Also, the book's observation that Joyce drew on Vico and Bruno is commonplace.

D66   Boyle, Robert, S. J.
JAMES JOYCE'S PAULINE VISION: A CATHOLIC EXPOSITION (Carbondale: Southern Illinois University Press, 1978)

The best work to date on Joyce's relation to Catholicism. Using the texts of Shakespeare, St Paul and Hopkins as important correlations, Boyle offers a brilliant analysis of Joyce's images to reveal intricately interladen texture and development of Joyce's themes. The trinitarian theme, for example, which assumes so much importance in *Ulysses*, is revealed by Boyle to be a vigorous and well-thought-out aspect of Joyce's aesthetic theory. Boyle's treatment of *Finnegans Wake* in the light of Pauline vision is also illuminating. Difficult to summarize because of the way ideas are developed, this work is an insightful and fascinating exegesis even for those to whom much of what Boyle says may seem remote. This study is a formidable response to those who view Joyce's work as a vindictive chronicle of his attempts to escape Catholicism, as well as to the apologetic view that Joyce never escaped the church's hold on him.

D67   Hodgart, Matthew
JAMES JOYCE: A STUDENT'S GUIDE (London: Routledge and Kegan Paul, 1978)

Though an ample introduction, this study is idiosyncratic, occasionally inaccurate and often arch.

D68   Kenner, Hugh
JOYCE'S VOICES (Berkeley and Los Angeles: University of California Press, 1978)

A brief but decisive study based on four T. S. Eliot Memorial Lectures delivered in 1975 at the University of Kent. The first chapter draws initially on Eliot's essay "*Ulysses*, Order and Myth", and Kenner focuses on objectivity and its effect on

Joyce's language. The second chapter coins a phrase that has become a standard term in Joyce criticism known as "The Uncle Charles Principle". It says, in brief, "that Joyce's fictions tend not to have a detached narrator though they seem to have". The two remaining chapters in *Joyce's Voices* also focus on Joyce's use of language and the varying voices that give energy and dimension to his text. The growing interest in narratology in contemporary criticism brings increasing attention to Kenner's seminal studies, but this is only one reason for the central position of his work in Joyce studies. The originality of his insights, the thoroughness of his arguments and his mastery of the entire modern period lie at the heart of his influence.

D69   MacCabe, Colin
JAMES JOYCE AND THE REVOLUTION OF THE
WORD (London: Macmillan, 1978)

Energetic and original study that comes out of the context of structuralism, Freud, Marx and Lacan. It gives new attention to Joyce's use of language and to how we read him. MacCabe's thesis has implications and extensions, especially political ones, that seem to push Joyce into political corners, but MacCabe's fresh examination of Joyce's work and the questions it raises about the relation between reader and text are critically important.

D70   Gluck, Barbara Reich
BECKETT AND JOYCE: FRIENDSHIP AND FICTION
(Lewisburg, Pa: Bucknell University Press, 1979)

Traces the complex relationship between Joyce and Beckett and the influence of Joyce on Beckett. Gluck's informative treatment of Beckett's trilogy demonstrates that Beckett uses themes of circularity, recurrence and time in much the same way as Joyce does. Deirdre Bair's biography, whatever its limitations, has given us considerable information about Beckett's close contact with Joyce between 1928 and 1932, but Gluck slights and even ignores some of Bair's revelations. There is a great deal in Gluck's book, but many aspects of the complicated Joyce–Beckett relationship, both literary and human, are still to be unravelled.

D71   Watson, George J.

IRISH IDENTITY AND THE LITERARY REVIVAL
(London: Croom Helm Ltd, 1979; New York: Barnes and
Noble, 1979)

This study looks at Yeats, Joyce, Synge and O'Casey in
relation to their "common context" during the last ten years of
the nineteenth century and the first thirty years of the
twentieth, focusing particularly on those events which reveal
the complex spectrum of political, social and religious
pressures that moulded the identity of Ireland during this
period. Watson's long chapter on Joyce is especially valuable
in providing an analysis of how Joyce's attitudes regarding the
relationship between private and public life were shaped by his
knowledge of Ireland's own fate during this long and difficult
period. Although Joyce was an early exile, Watson shows that
he was hardly indifferent to the fate of Ireland.

D72   Benstock, Shari and Bernard Benstock, eds
WHO'S HE WHEN HE'S AT HOME? A JAMES JOYCE
DIRECTORY (Urbana: University of Illinois Press, 1980)

A work of careful scholarship and great industry, the
Directory lists and discusses over 3,000 personages who
appear in Joyce's work—mythical, fictional, legendary,
historical and anonymous. All Joyce's work is covered except
Finnegans Wake, which is served by Adaline Glasheen's *Third
Census of Finnegans Wake*. Presented in a clear format with
carefully prepared introductions, the Benstocks' work has
many uses. Omissions appear non-existent, even to the
"singing cake of soap" in "Circe". The introduction, also of
great value, discusses the use of names and particular
problems associated with each work and with each episode in
Ulysses. Also provided are appendices entitled "The Joycean
Method of Cataloguing" and "Molly's Masculine Pronouns".

D73   Brivic, Sheldon
JOYCE BETWEEN FREUD AND JUNG (Port
Washington, N.Y.: Kennikat Press, 1980)

Investigates all Joyce's work from the psychoanalytic point of
view and attempts to trace Joyce's mental process through his
works. The contributions to psychoanalytic theory by such
thinkers as Klein, Lacan and Winnicott are recognized by
Brivic, perhaps even exploited. Brivic's study is expansive and
flexible, his methodology eclectic. He examines *A Portrait*

from a Freudian perspective, goes on to connect the unconscious determinants of Joyce's personality to his sense of meaning and value (Brivic would say "system"), and concludes with an examination of Joyce's mythology in terms of Jungian analysis. Brivic's prose is frequently dense and a bit unrelieved, but the work as a whole is solid, insightful and well-informed.

D74   Gillespie, Michael Patrick
INVERTED VOLUMES IMPROPERLY ARRANGED: JAMES JOYCE AND HIS TRIESTE LIBRARY (Ann Arbor: UMI Research Press, 1980)

Attempts to reconstruct the working library of Joyce during the years of his artistic maturation, 1904–20. This book, while providing a theoretical list of books Joyce may have referred to or consulted, falls short on a detailed analysis of Joyce's reaction to these sources or their place within the intellectual milieu of Joyce's day.

D75   Kiely, Robert
BEYOND EGOTISM: THE FICTION OF JAMES JOYCE, VIRGINIA WOOLF, AND D. H. LAWRENCE (Cambridge, Mass.: Harvard University Press, 1980)

The first study to treat this literary triangle in any detailed and extended way. Kiely concentrates on the convergence of several themes but particularly on the role of the ego in the relationship between author and reader, between character and author, and among characters in a given work. It is from this perspective that Kiely explores these writers' similarities. Although his angle seems confining at times, it yields some interesting common ground on which to view the three novelists.

D76   Manganiello, Dominic
JOYCE'S POLITICS (London: Routledge and Kegan Paul, 1980)

Interesting and thorough study of Joyce's political thinking as it is reflected in his life and works, especially the political aspects of Joyce's work that were informed by continental sources and events. Manganiello's study blunts some of the easy assumptions in Joyce criticism that he cared little for politics or political theory unless it was Irish. Manganiello is extremely well informed in political thought and the extent and ways in which Joyce absorbed these ideas, and he is convincing in his analysis of Joyce's eclectic assimilation and demonstration of political thought in his work.

D77   Cope, Jackson I.
JOYCE'S CITIES: ARCHAEOLOGIES OF THE SOUL
(Baltimore: Johns Hopkins University Press, 1981)

Treats Joyce's imaginative vision of the family and its extension into the city. According to Cope this vision is rooted in the Victorian consciousness but with antecedents stretching back to ancient texts, cultures and mystical philosophies. Cope makes convincing points on the influence on Joyce of D'Annunzio, Irish hermetic societies, Christian cabalism and Egyptian religion. The author stresses Joyce's irony and scepticism regarding the supernatural. The valuable aspect of this book is the analysis of Joyce's transformation in *Dubliners* and *Ulysses* of the Victorian image of the family and the city.

D78   Gordon, John
JAMES JOYCE'S METAMORPHOSES (Dublin: Gill and Macmillan, 1981; Totowa, N.J.: Barnes and Noble, 1981)

Explores the premise that Joyce based his art on the constant merging of the exterior world with our contemporary selves. Gordon traces this process in all the major writings of Joyce, from *Chamber Music* to *Finnegans Wake*. His analysis demonstrates that much of the radical change in Joyce's style is the result of the author's reflections on *how* he observed the world, applying that knowledge to understanding his own specific place, time and personality. Gordon also makes an argument for the technical continuity of *Ulysses* and *Finnegans Wake*, concluding that the latter only carries on Joyce's preoccupation with the way the mind works.

D79   Reynolds, Mary T.
JOYCE AND DANTE: THE SHAPING IMAGINATION
(Princeton: Princeton University Press, 1981)

A source study not only of Dante's influence on Joyce but on how reading Joyce refines our knowledge of Dante. Among the topics covered is an account of the stages of development

Joyce passed through in his reading of Dante. Chapters are also devoted to the importance of paternal figures in both Joyce and Dante and to the theme of love in both authors, exploring two of Dante's lovers, Paolo and Francesca, who especially appealed to Joyce. Later in the book, Reynolds focuses on what she calls lustration patterns, Joyce's use of the ritual aspects of myth as metaphor. A final chapter concerns Joyce's major fiction—*A Portrait, Ulysses, Finnegans Wake*—and gives a consecutive rendering of Dante's effects on Joyce. An appendix is included that contains all allusions to Dante in Joyce's work. Since the Dante perspective is so crucial to Joyce studies, this book provides a necessary and knowledgeable source study.

D80   Benstock, Bernard, ed.
THE SEVENTH OF JOYCE (Brighton, England: Harvester Press, 1982; Bloomington, Indiana: Indiana University Press, 1982)

A collection of papers from the Seventh International Joyce Symposium held in Zurich. Included are essays on all major works of Joyce and an especially wide variety of comparative studies of Joyce and other writers such as Beckett, Freud and Faulkner. Also represented are treatments of narrative theory, Joyce and Judaism, sexual attitudes, and elements of modern science in *Ulysses* and *Finnegans Wake*.

D81   Bushrui, Suheil Badi, and Bernard Benstock, eds
JAMES JOYCE: AN INTERNATIONAL PERSPECTIVE: CENTENARY ESSAYS IN HONOR OF THE LATE SIR DESMOND COCHRANE, IRISH LITERARY STUDIES 10 (Gerrards Cross, England: Colin Smythe, 1982; Totowa, New Jersey: Barnes and Noble, 1982)

These centenary essays cover such topics as trusting textual evidence in *Ulysses*, the poetry of Joyce, intra-referentiality between Joyce texts and subtexts, and a review of current research. Also included are reviews of Joyce scholarship in the Netherlands, Switzerland and Germany, as well as an account of Joyce in the Arab world. This is an international collaboration of scholarship that reveals Joyce's stature as a major figure of world literature.

D82   Eco, Umberto
       THE AESTHETICS OF CHAOSMOS: THE MIDDLE
       AGES OF JAMES JOYCE, trans. Ellen Esrock, University
       of Tulsa Monograph Series, 18 (Tulsa, Oklahoma: University
       of Tulsa, 1982)

This monograph treats the conflict in Joyce between his sympathy for the medieval order of experience and his need for a twentieth-century sensibility. Eco explores this conflict in the early Joyce to reveal an artist striving to replace an old order but confined by traditional definitions of art. *Ulysses*, also, by dissolving and recreating the technique of the novel, reflects the chaos of the modern world, yet still remains within a traditional sensibility. Only *Finnegans Wake* offers a complete break with tradition to achieve a completely non-representational world, an artistic vision most closely related to the medieval rejection of realism. Eco's thesis is that Joyce's struggle with technique led him back to the medieval, Aristotelian perspective, creating in *Finnegans Wake* a work as thoroughly medieval as the Book of Kells. The strength of Eco's book is his extensive background in classical and medieval studies and semiotics.

D83   Epstein, Edmund L., ed.
       A STARCHAMBER QUIRY: A JAMES JOYCE
       CENTENNIAL VOLUME, 1882–1982 (London and New
       York: Methuen, 1982)

Contains five essays by distinguished critics on various themes of modernism in Joyce. Hugh Kenner focuses on a mechanical rather than an intellectual impetus for modernism, examining how the urban environment and the machine have affected consciousness. Fritz Senn explores how interpretation of Joyce has become so schematized as to overlook the most important aspect of his work, the discrepancies which disrupt textual symmetries. Edmund L. Epstein's essay explains Joyce's use of the body to emblemize the aspiration of the soul. Robert Boyle reveals the submerged yet operative dimension of Joyce's Catholicism, stating that Joyce continues a belief in the mystery of the Trinity that began with St Paul. Clive Hart recommends a rapid and simple reading of the *Wake*, paying as much attention to the surface as possible. Hart insists that after decades of detailed explication, the need is now to grasp the impact of the whole, reading the *Wake* in terms of the everyday world.

D84   Hedberg, Johannes, *et al.*
NORDIC REJOYCINGS 1982: IN COMMEMORATION OF THE CENTENARY OF THE BIRTH OF JAMES JOYCE (Sweden: James Joyce Society of Sweden and Finland, 1982)

A collection of nine essays by members of the James Joyce Society of Sweden and Finland that illustrates well the conventional strain of Nordic Joyce criticism. "The Nordic joyrides seem to have one feature in common, a certain level-headed approach, a bias towards usefulness and factual clarity," Fritz Senn writes in the Afterword. Senn provides an accurate assessment of this collection which deals with the problems of translating Joyce into Finnish, Joyce's attempts to establish a cinema, allusions to Yeats in Joyce's first two novels, and Joyce's concern with language, among other topics. A useful bibliography of James Joyce's works published in Danish, Finnish and Swedish is included.

D85   Henke, Suzette and Elaine Unkeless, eds
WOMEN IN JOYCE (Urbana: University of Illinois Press, 1982)

The focus for this collection of essays is to examine the topic of female presence in Joyce and how his treatment of women reflects, verifies or criticizes prevalent beliefs about women. Florence L. Walzl uses sociological statistics to explain the limited opportunities for women in *Dubliners*. Suzette Henke analyses the Oedipal and Manichean aspects of Stephen. Henke also offers an original insight into the plight of Gerty MacDowell as a victim of the media. Margot Norris and Shari Benstock analyse women figures in the *Wake*, specifically Issy and Anna Livia Plurabelle. Robert Boyle interprets the arrangement of poems in *Chamber Music* to represent the rise and fall of a love affair. Elaine Unkeless attempts to interpret Molly as something other than sex symbol or archetypal earth mother. This volume represents a trend towards looking at Joyce as a "female writer", yet also explores his limitations in articulating feminine vision.

D86   List, Robert N.
DEDALUS IN HARLEM: THE JOYCE–ELLISON

CONNECTION (Washington, D.C.: University Press of America, 1982)

This book explores various Joycean influences on black writing in America, focusing on Ralph Ellison. The thesis is the commonality of Irish and black experience. The study, however, is flawed by numerous errors in interpretation and organization, presenting a very superficial reading of Joyce and a social and political analysis that is poorly developed and simplistic.

D87   Martin, Stoddard
       WAGNER TO THE WASTE LAND: A STUDY OF THE
       RELATIONSHIP OF WAGNER TO ENGLISH
       LITERATURE. (London: Macmillan, 1982; Totowa, N.J.:
       Barnes and Noble, 1982)

Martin's title gives a precise description of this study which traces Wagner's considerable influence upon many major modern writers. His thirty-three page chapter on Joyce presents a skilful reading of Wagnerian echoes in Joyce's work, although it is weakened somewhat as Martin tries to do too much in too little space. This produces an effect more like cataloguing than thoughtful, incisive analysis. In this general treatment, Joyce's progression from an early reverence for Wagner, to a mid-career disdain, and finally to a later stance of gentle mocking is made quite clear. Martin is careful to point out that Wagner's greatest impact on Joyce lies not in allusion and motif, but rather in the similarity of artistic goals. He argues, furthermore, that Joyce derived important aspects of his narrative technique from the model offered by Wagner's music.

D88   McCabe, Colin, ed.
       JAMES JOYCE: NEW PERSPECTIVES (Brighton,
       England: Harvester Press, 1982; Bloomington: Indiana
       University Press, 1982)

A collection of lectures given at Cambridge that includes pieces by the following: Fritz Senn, who encourages critics to develop new lines of response to Joycean text; Colin MacCabe, who reduces *Finnegans Wake* to a fundamental narrative core; Patrick Parrinder, who addresses the negative reaction of European contemporaries to Joyce's later work; and Raymond Williams, who writes on *Exiles* and Joyce and

Ibsen. In addition, Maria Jolas questions accepted notions of Joyce's strong dependence on women, and Jean-Michel Rabaté interprets *Dubliners* in terms of post-structural concepts of textual silence and absence.

D89   McCormack, W. J. and Alistair Stead, eds
        JAMES JOYCE AND MODERN LITERATURE (London
        and Boston: Routledge and Kegan Paul, 1982)

A collection of essays drawn from the Leeds Centenary Conference, this volume shows the relation of Joyce's work to modernism, history, literary tradition and narrative theory. Peter Bekker's essay is noteworthy for its sound inspection of the reading process behind *Finnegans Wake*. Timothy Webb explores Joyce's relationship to the Romantics, particularly Shelley. Fredric Jameson's essay stresses a need in the Joyce community (himself an outsider) to undermine constantly reading assumptions.

D90   Werner, Craig Hansen
        PARADOXICAL RESOLUTIONS: AMERICAN
        FICTION SINCE JAMES JOYCE (Urbana: University of
        Illinois Press, 1982)

This book explores Joyce's influence as a realistic and romantic writer on American writers as diverse as Faulkner, Kerouac, Plath and Pynchon. Although the general premise of the study has value, Werner does not define sharply enough the specific themes and techniques Joyce has contributed to American writers.

D91   Church, Margaret
        STRUCTURE AND THEME: DON QUIXOTE TO
        JAMES JOYCE (Columbus: Ohio State University Press,
        1983)

An analysis of structural components of thirteen novels. Includes two chapters related to Joyce. "How the Vicociclometer works: The Fiction of James Joyce" examines the "gradually unfolding Viconian pattern" which appears in Joyce's earlier work (*Dubliners* and *Portrait*). In "Joycean Structure in *Jacob's Room* and *Mrs Dalloway*", Joyce's impact on Virginia Woolf's theory of literary composition is outlined. "Whereas Flaubert had been for Joyce a powerful catalyst informing Joyce's concept of the craft of fiction, it was ironically Joyce himself, perhaps, who acted as an early catalyst for Virginia Woolf's sense of form in the novel."

D92   Halper, Nathan
        STUDIES IN JOYCE (Ann Arbor, Mich.: UMI Research
        Press, 1983)

        A collection of miscellaneous essays on Joyce's major works, especially *Finnegans Wake.* Halper is an outstanding example of a non-professional Joycean dedicated to clarity of response and common sense. Included in this book are Halper's explication of a code between Joyce and Pound, his reflections on Joyce's dictation of *Finnegans Wake* to Samuel Beckett; and his account of his meeting with Edmund Wilson. These essays represent the author's lifelong observations on Joyce.

D93   Peterson, Richard F., Alan M. Cohn and Edmund L.
        Epstein, eds
        WORK IN PROGRESS: JOYCE CENTENARY ESSAYS
        (Carbondale: Southern Illinois University Press, 1983)

        A collection of essays representing thematic readings of Joyce's major works and more general approaches to specific concerns among them. Patrick A. McCarthy's essay on *Finnegans Wake* and its dynamic relationship with the reading process and Robert Boyle's discussion of Joyce's often-complex relationship with religious faith stand out among the others. The essays by Sheldon Brivic and Margaret Church also offer valuable surveys of critical reception on various points of contention regarding Joyce's work. The diverse backgrounds offer a representative spectrum of approaches to Joyce ranging from the New Criticism to the newer criticisms.

D94   Quillian, William H.
        . HAMLET AND THE NEW POETIC: JAMES JOYCE
        AND T. S. ELIOT, Studies in Modern Literature, 13 (Ann
        Arbor, Michigan: UMI Research Press, 1983)

        Quillian sees Eliot's and Joyce's rejection of Hamlet as a decisive point in the making of the modernistic poetic, a response with roots in Mallarmé and Laforgue's demystification of Hamlet by the use of irony. Quillian views Eliot and Joyce as breaking the three-century obsession with Hamlet as a figure of doubt and hesitation.

D95   Riquelme, John Paul
        TELLER AND TALE IN JOYCE'S FICTION:
        OSCILLATING PERSPECTIVES (Baltimore: Johns
        Hopkins University Press, 1983)

        This study is an attempt to unite the major works of Joyce
        under a single explanatory model, that of the "oscillating
        perspective". The author defines this concept as a system of
        self-interfering elements that fluctuate in a Joycean text
        between mutually defining poles. The author uses quasi-
        mathematical models such as a Mobius Strip to demonstrate
        how the text builds meaning into the consciousness of the
        reader by doublings, repetitions and transformations in the
        narrative. This study focuses on a single plane of inquiry in a
        way that would appeal to the non-specialist as well as
        specialist.

D96   Wright, David G.
        CHARACTERS IN JOYCE (Dublin: Gill and Macmillan,
        1983; Totowa, N.J.: Barnes and Noble, 1983)

        The author of this work contends that textual puzzles in Joyce
        are clarified by looking at the real people behind the fictional
        characters, especially at the author himself. Wright covers
        each of Joyce's major works, drawing parallels between
        characters such as Stephen Dedalus and aspects of Joyce's
        personality. The author, however, examines only biographical
        speculations already well covered and provides no new
        information or a critical method sound enough to stimulate
        interest in his approach.

D97   Attridge, Derek and Daniel Ferrer, eds
        POST-STRUCTURALIST JOYCE: ESSAYS FROM THE
        FRENCH (Cambridge and New York: Cambridge University
        Press, 1984)

        These essays, translated here into English, offer a combination
        of studies in both Joyce and contemporary literary theory
        without necessarily privileging one over the other. They
        appeared previously in predominantly Parisian journals over
        the last twenty years and present a representative sample of a
        distinctly "French" (but surprisingly conservative at times)
        approach to both subjects. As the editors point out in their
        introduction, Joyce offers a near-ideal testing-ground for

contemporary theory, and "the affinity between Joyce and the theory of the Text and the Subject being elaborated in Paris is so close that it is not likely to dry up soon." Among the contributions are essays by Stephen Heath, Jacques Aubert, Hélène Cixous and Jacques Derrida, although even the essay by Derrida seems, surprisingly, to lean more toward the fairly conventional readings of Joyce rather than toward the deconstruction one might expect.

D98   Bowen, Zack, and James F. Carens, eds
       A COMPANION TO JOYCE STUDIES (Westport, Conn.:
       Greenwood Press, 1984)

This 818-page collection offers a thorough overview of Joyce studies. The sixteen essays and two appendices (on Joyce's names and library manuscript holdings) by a number of well-known critics cover his life, major and minor works, and critical writings, as well as offering a description of the development of Joyce scholarship over the last forty-five years. The substantial critical treatments of Joyce's work presented here will provide a thorough introduction, with items of interest even to the more seasoned Joyce scholar. Florence L. Walzl's work on *Dubliners*, Bowen's discussions of *Ulysses*, and three individual essays on *Finnegans Wake* by Patrick McCarthy, Michael Begnal and Barbara DiBernard stand out in this regard. Also included are useful essays on Joyce's verse (Chester G. Anderson), *Stephen Hero* (Thomas E. Connolly), and *Exiles* (Bernard Benstock).

D99   Dennison, Sally
       (ALTERNATIVE) LITERARY PUBLISHING: FIVE
       MODERN HISTORIES (Iowa City: University of Iowa
       Press, 1984)

Traces the strong connection between modernism and alternative forms of publishing, with a highly detailed chapter on Joyce. Also deals with four other significant modernists (Eliot, Woolf, Nin and Nabokov). The distinctly iconoclastic nature of these writers' works made publication particularly difficult, and Dennison succeeds in establishing connections between this difficulty and its influence on modern literature. Although Dennison draws only on previously published sources, the context of her study makes the chapter on Joyce interesting.

D100   Ehrlich, Heyward, ed.
         LIGHT RAYS: JAMES JOYCE AND MODERNISM (New
         York: New Horizon Press, 1984)

A much-needed collection of essays which deals with Joyce's work in relation to other branches of modernism. It includes approaches to Joyce from the perspectives of popular culture, experimental literature, the new sexuality, contemporary philosophy, neoteric psychology, avant-garde music and abstract art by such well-known writers as Fritz Senn, Richard Ellmann, Margot Norris, Robert Boyle, Leslie Fiedler, Hugh Kenner and Zack Bowen. Also included are musical scores by John Cage and Pierre Boulez related to Joyce's work, examinations of Matisse's etchings for *Ulysses*, Ad Reinhardt's cartoon relating to *Portrait*, as well as more unconventional criticism by Cage, Ihab Hassan and Norman O. Brown. A highly useful book that covers a broad range of topics related both to Joyce and modernism in general.

D101   Loss, Archie K.
         JOYCE'S VISIBLE ART: THE WORK OF JOYCE AND
         THE VISUAL ARTS 1904-1922 (Ann Arbor, Michigan:
         UMI Research Press, 1984)

Illustrates connections between nineteenth-century visual arts and Joyce's symbolism and technique. Asserts that Joyce's "visual imagery [was] fixed in the world of that time, so that ever afterwards, in spite of his ignorance of painting, his imagery reflected the *fin-de-siècle* way of seeing (if not always interpreting) the world." Includes forty illustrations of influential paintings, etchings, woodcuts, etc. Weakened by its omission of *Finnegans Wake*.

D102   Melchiori, Georgio
         JOYCE IN ROME: THE GENESIS OF *ULYSSES* (Rome:
         Bulzoni Editore, 1984)

Contains essays arguing that the seven months Joyce spent in Rome, 1906-7, did not produce a creative dearth as most critics assume, but added richly to Joyce's repertoire of creative ideas. Political and historical dimensions are covered by Dominic Manganiello, Seamus Deane, Joan Fitzgerald, Diamuid Maguire and Carlo Bigazzi. Speculations on the literary genesis of *Ulysses* and "The Dead" are covered by

Georgio Melchiori and Franca Ruggieri, respectively. Biographical aspects of Joyce's stay in Rome are presented by Carla de Petris and Franco Onarati, who present original research into Joyce's Roman itinerary and activity as a bank clerk.

D103 Moscato, Michael and Leslie LeBlanc, eds
THE UNITED STATES OF AMERICA v. ONE BOOK
ENTITLED *ULYSSES* BY JAMES JOYCE:
DOCUMENTS AND COMMENTARY—A FIFTY-YEAR
RETROSPECTIVE (Frederick, Md: University Publications
of America, 1984)

This book, with an introduction by Richard Ellmann, makes available the legal materials surrounding the *Ulysses* litigation in America. It also casts light on the story of the American publication of *Ulysses,* beginning with its 1918 serialization in *The Little Review.* There are eighteen commentaries which precede the document section. These include articles, editorials and journal articles about the *Ulysses* trial and aspects of censoring literature. The document section includes Document 191, Judge Woolsey's opinion that "*Ulysses* may, therefore, be admitted into the United States." Following this is Document 193, the cable of congratulations on the outcome of the case from Bennet A. Cerf of Random House to Paul Léon, Joyce's friend and adviser. This material is not only valuable for the publication history, but it is also an important cultural and legal document that reflects the consciousness of a period.

D104 Parrinder, Patrick
JAMES JOYCE (Cambridge and New York: Cambridge
University Press, 1984)

A survey covering Joyce's major works, although Parrinder is clearly uncomfortable with *Finnegans Wake*, as he devotes little more than introductory material to it as compared with his elaborate, five-part study of *Ulysses.* Following a substantial biographical and critical discussion of Joyce's work up to his last two novels, detailed historical/theoretical analyses of *Ulysses* and, to a far lesser extent, *Finnegans Wake*, are given. Parrinder suggests that a difficulty in reading *Finnegans Wake* lies in justifying certain readings over others, an assertion which flattens somewhat the clearly radical gesture that *Finnegans Wake* embodies regarding the notion of conventional readings. This study, however, is a sound general reading of Joyce's canon that incorporates recent critical thought.

D105   Scott, Bonnie Kime
JOYCE AND FEMINISM (Bloomington: Indiana
University Press, 1984)

This study offers a broad feminist framework for Joyce's life and art, beginning by providing historical background and concentrating on Joyce's early encounters with feminist movements, both cultural and literary. After discussing the intellectual milieu which possibly shaped Joyce's attitudes, Scott considers the women of Joyce's family (mother, sisters, wife) looking at them carefully and determining their relationships—especially as those relationships shaped and formed his understanding and attitudes towards women. Scott provides a valuable reflection on female critics of Joyce such as Mary Colum, Rebecca West, and Virginia Woolf as well as later feminist interpretations. At the heart of her work, however, are her own readings of Emma from *A Portrait*, Molly Bloom, and Issy in *Finnegans Wake*. This study analyses Joyce's work from a variety of feminist perspectives, and its breadth and background make it an important contribution to this perspective and to Joyce criticism generally.

D106   Senn, Fritz
JOYCE'S DISLOCUTIONS: ESSAYS ON READING AS
TRANSLATION, ed. John Paul Riquelme (Baltimore: Johns
Hopkins University Press, 1984)

This collection of essays by an important European critic represents a method of reading Joyce based on translating principles. Senn emphasizes that Joyce's use of language parallels a process whereby meaning is derived by verbal substitution, tracing semantic relationships between words and disrupting the linguistic field of reference as if translating. These essays draw on philological subtlety and multi-lingualism as a reading procedure. Senn's essays have been highly influential and this volume is important in that it brings most of them together and allows the reader to see better the development of Senn's thought.

D107   Benstock, Bernard
JAMES JOYCE (New York: Frederick Ungar, 1985)

A solid, introductory study of Joyce's work in Ungar's Literature and Life Series which offers a good contemporary perspective. Inclusion of a chapter devoted to *Exiles* makes valuable commentary on an often-underrated work. A detailed chronology of events in Joyce's life provides a useful complement to the historical/literary background Benstock establishes to create a sense of milieu for the general reader. Because Benstock provides a nice sketch of the period, his study would also be of interest to those concerned with the development of literary modernism in general.

D108   Benstock, Bernard
CRITICAL ESSAYS ON JAMES JOYCE (Boston: G. K. Hall, 1985)

An historical anthology of Joyce criticism, ranging from classic "Early Assessments" (essays by Pound, Wells, Eliot and Wilson), to "Coterie and Pioneers" (Beckett, Gilbert and Budgen), to conventional, "Mainstream" studies, (Kain, Ellmann, Kenner, Senn, etc.) to the newer, less-conventional studies, "Nouvelles Critiques" (Iser, Staley, Norris, Shari Benstock, etc.). Also contains a helpful introductory essay by Benstock, "Assimilating James Joyce", which attempts to place Joyce studies in a broader literary context. Valuable for studying developments in Joyce criticism as well as for its handy collection of well-known essays by different and respected Joyce critics finally offered between the same two covers.

D109   Brown, Richard
JAMES JOYCE AND SEXUALITY (Cambridge and New York: Cambridge University Press, 1985)

Explores the subject of sexuality in Joyce as a direct statement on the contemporary context in which he lived. The author attempts to explore and define a specific Joycean attitude towards sexual mores that is representative of a modern outlook. By careful attention to Joyce's subject matter relating to love and marriage, to sexual pleasure over procreation, to the scientific interest in sexuality and to women, Brown interprets Joyce as a radical philosopher of sexuality, his works a challenge to traditional notions of human sexual conduct. This book is worthwhile for its thorough scholarship on the background of reading and reflection that informed Joyce's opinions on sexuality, and for offering a forthright treatment of a subject that is often neglected or conveniently dismissed.

D110   Deane, Seamus
CELTIC REVIVALS: ESSAYS IN MODERN IRISH LITERATURE 1880–1980 (London and Boston: Faber and Faber, 1985)

Two of Deane's essays on Joyce in this volume, which broadly covers one hundred years of Irish literature from 1880–1980, are especially well-argued and richly informed discussions of Joyce's art. His first essay, "Joyce and Stephen: The Provincial Intellectual", addresses Joyce's unique construction of his hero in *A Portrait* and *Ulysses*. The second essay, "Joyce and Nationalism", is a brief but highly provocative commentary on the relationship of Joyce's work to Irish history and politics. Far from simply repudiating Irish nationalism, Deane argues that Joyce incorporated Ireland as a cultural and political entity in all its mutations "as a model of the world and, more importantly, as a model of the fictive. In revealing the essentially fictive nature of political imagining, Joyce did not repudiate Irish nationalism."

D111   Schlossman, Beryl
JOYCE'S CATHOLIC COMEDY OF LANGUAGE (Madison: University of Wisconsin Press, 1985)

Identifies the substantial role that Irish Catholicism plays primarily in *A Portrait, Ulysses* and *Finnegans Wake*. While tracing liturgical and theological elements of Joyce's work, Schlossman produces a skilful reading of the dichotomous relationship Joyce had with his Catholic background. Her use of contemporary theory, especially those branches associated with Jacques Lacan, contributes substantially to her investigation of the psychological, philosophical and semiotic concerns that Joyce displayed in his work and that figured so significantly in his symbolic structures. Schlossman also provides a useful appendix on *The Book of Kells*, Irish illuminated writing and their importance to Joyce.

D112   Herr, Cheryl
        JOYCE'S ANATOMY OF CULTURE (Urbana and
        Chicago: University of Illinois Press, 1986)

This book combines semiotic and Marxist interpretations with substantial scholarship on Irish popular culture. By exploring the forms of discourse in the newspaper, the stage and the sermon, the author analyses and links the socio-historical forces of culture that have shaped Joyce's art from *Dubliners* to *Finnegans Wake*. Herr's thesis opposes the critic who maintains Joyce is neither didactic nor political. By concentrating on institutions rather than individuals, she presents a Joyce whose subtle insights into contradictions, repressions and distortions imposed by the British ruling class, the Catholic Church and various censoring bodies make him an essentially political writer. With her emphasis on placing Joyce in a wide cultural and historical context, the author can be seen as extending the political thesis set forth by Richard Ellmann and later by Dominic Manganiello. This book provides a welcome alternative to the recent critical emphasis on narrative and style, at the same time stressing that popular culture was for Joyce not only a source of artistic formations, but a means of expressing an intense anatomy of Irish political forces. Included is a bibliography for the study of Irish popular culture.

D113   O'Shea, Michael J.
        JAMES JOYCE AND HERALDRY (Albany: State
        University of New York Press, 1986)

A thorough and fairly rigorous investigation of heraldic elements in Joyce's work in general and more specifically in *A Portrait, Ulysses* and *Finnegans Wake*. O'Shea provides insight into the symbolic correlatives of Joyce's heraldic references which undoubtedly puzzle even seasoned readers. This study is not merely another concordance, however, since O'Shea strives successfully to illustrate the ways that Joyce utilized and transformed heraldry. O'Shea succeeds in arming the reader with an informed accounting of heraldry, as well as clearing up misinformation generated by less cautious critical works on Joyce. A useful glossary of heraldry in Joyce's work is included as an appendix.

D114   Scott, Bonnie Kime
         JAMES JOYCE (Atlantic Highlands, N.J.: Humanities
         Press, 1987)

This work is an extension of Scott's earlier study, *Joyce and Feminism*, in which she "presented feminist historical and biographical backgrounds for Joyce" as well as extended analysis of female characters. *James Joyce*, in the "Feminist Readings Series", continues Scott's study of female characters in Joyce, adding Gretta Conroy, Bertha Rowan, Beatrice Justice, Gerty MacDowell and ALP. The author also applies feminist analysis to Stephen and Simon Dedalus. The work is more theoretical in conception than her earlier volume and applies a matrix of feminine theory to Joyce's texts. This plurality yields to interesting interpretations and reveals a wide variety of feminist approaches. For all its theoretical discussion, Scott's study is especially interesting for its conscious demonstration of feminist critical applications and fresh analysis. Scott explores the significant aspects of feminist criticism as it pertains to the work of Joyce. These aspects include a discussion of male and female differences, how discourse and behaviour are largely determined by a patriarchal code, and how Joyce both powerfully represents and challenges this male code that is culturally predominant. Although the author admits that her study is not theoretically pure in its adherence to a single feminist school, her approach to Joyce is through a number of current theoretical models— all of which reflect a concern with feminist perspective.

D115   Verene, Donald Phillip, ed.
         VICO AND JOYCE (Albany, N.Y.: State University of New
         York Press, 1987)

A collection of essays dealing with many aspects of the Joyce–Vico relationship. The essays in this volume were occasioned by the international conference held in Venice in 1985 on Vico and Joyce. The volume is divided into three sections, "Cycla and History", "Joyce and Vico" and "Language and Myth", and includes an epilogue by the editor that provides a good overview of the relationship between Vico and Joyce. Among contributors are Northrop Frye, Mary T. Reynolds, Rosa Maria Bosinelli and Peter Munz. The general quality of these sixteen essays is quite high and collectively they form a broad picture of the many-faceted relationship between the works of Vico and Joyce.

Articles and Chapters in Books

D116   Connolly, Cyril
"The Position of Joyce", *Life and Letters*, 2:8 (1929), 273–290; also in CONDEMNED PLAYGROUND: ESSAYS: 1927–1944 (London: Routledge, 1945; New York: Macmillan, 1946), pp. 1–15

An early assessment by an informed critic on the place of *Ulysses* in the modern novel.

D117   Wilson, Edmund L.
"James Joyce", AXEL'S CASTLE: A STUDY OF THE IMAGINATIVE LITERATURE OF 1870–1930 (New York and London: Scribner's, 1931), pp. 191–236

The first important assessment of Joyce's achievement and remains a seminal contribution to the criticism of modern literature as well as to Joyce studies. Wilson's chapter on Joyce is far more than an introduction; he places Joyce in the context of European literature and its modern development and, while stressing Joyce's originality and imagination, illustrates how his methods and techniques are a part of a larger "modern" imagination that grew out of French symbolism and the realistic tradition of Flaubert.

D118   Broch, Hermann
"Joyce and the Present Age" (1936), trans. Eugene Jolas and Maria Jolas, A JAMES JOYCE YEARBOOK, ed. Maria Jolas (Paris: Transition Press, 1949), pp. 60–108

Broch, a leading figure of the time in Austrian letters, praises Joyce for the capacity of his art to participate in the universal and also express the age of which he is part. Yet Broch also faults Joyce for his pessimism and negation of rational thought and clear language, aspects which he sees as destroying the power of expression in *Finnegans Wake*.

D119   Miller, Henry
"The Universe of Death", *Phoenix*, 1:1 (1938), 33–64

Notes that Joyce in *Ulysses* reveals his "perpetual frantic search for God". An interesting essay for its harsh condemnation of Joyce by Miller, speaking as a successor to D.H. Lawrence. Joyce is described as pathological, maladjusted, and corrupted by philosophical and sexual perversity.

D120   Slochower, Harry
"In Quest of Everyman: James Joyce", NO VOICE IS WHOLLY LOST ... : WRITERS AND THINKERS IN WAR AND PEACE (London: Dobson, 1943; New York: Creative Age Press, 1945), pp. 243–48

An early Marxist approach to modern literature, which sees Joyce's break from earlier traditions as only partial. Of interest because it reflects an important milieu in which Joyce's works were received.

D121   Baker, James R.
"James Joyce: Esthetic Freedom and Dramatic Art", *Western Humanities Review*, 5 (1950–1), 29–40

This essay unifies the theoretical concepts of aesthetics found in three crucial works of Joyce: the manuscript of *Stephen Hero*, *A Portrait*, and excerpts from Joyce's early notebooks. These works share, with varying degrees of confidence, an aesthetic impulse in Joyce to escape the common sensibility. (Reprinted in G3.)

D122   Ussher, Arland
"James Joyce: Doubting Thomist and Joking Jesuit", THREE GREAT IRISHMEN: SHAW, YEATS AND JOYCE (London: Gollancz, 1952), pp. 115–60

Although Ussher finds *Finnegans Wake* to be Joyce's failure, he concentrates on Joyce's use of comedy with special reference to the *Wake* within the Irish tradition.

D123   Cope, Jackson, I.
"James Joyce: Test Case for a Theory of Style", *Journal of English Literary History*, 21 (1954), 221–36

Written as an affront to both structural and historical criticism, Cope offers a humanistic response to bridging literary form and experience. The author's thesis is that style is a direct impression of the structure of thought, and that close stylistic analysis gives not only the shape of a writer's mind but clues to the shape of his culture.

D124　Russell, Francis
"Joyce and Alexandria", THREE STUDIES IN TWENTIETH CENTURY OBSCURITY (Aldington, Kent, England: Hand and Flower Press, 1954), pp. 7–44

This study, however wrong-headed, gives a glimpse of a common reaction to Joyce in the relatively early days. Russell sees Joyce's work reflecting the "cultural void" rather than striking out against it.

D125　Tindall, William York
FORCES IN MODERN BRITISH LITERATURE, 1885–1956 (New York: Knopf, 1956), passim

This study stresses political alignments and their relationship to modern British literature. Tindall treats Joyce within a variety of literary and political contexts.

D126　Seward, Barbara
"Joyce and Synthesis", THE SYMBOLIC ROSE (New York: Columbia University Press, 1960), pp. 187–221

An extended study of Joyce's use of rose symbolism in his work, especially good in noting the rose as a structural symbol in *A Portrait*.

D127　Heppenstall, Rayner
"Streams of Consciousness", THE FOURFOLD TRADITION: NOTES ON THE FRENCH AND ENGLISH LITERATURES (New York: New Directions, 1961) pp. 132–59

A brief comparison of Joyce and D. H. Lawrence is followed by a discussion of Dujardin's *Les Lauriers sont coupés* and its influence on Joyce's narrative technique in *Ulysses*. Heppenstall's argument is that the bold narrative experiment in stream-of-consciousness in the first half of the book was marred by Joyce's excess experimentation in the latter part, which is attributed to nervous fatigue and boredom. The author then speculates that only the removal of whole chapters would have created a consistent narrative structure and saved *Ulysses* from artistic disaster. *Finnegans Wake* is summarily dismissed.

D128   Noon, William T., S.J.
"James Joyce: Unfacts, Fiction, and Facts", *PMLA*, 76 (1961), 254–76

Noon cautions against close autobiographical readings of Joyce's fiction even though Joyce used his life for much of his material. In spite of the fact that Noon and many other critics stressed the distance between Joyce and his fictional character Stephen Dedalus, it is not an uncommon error to appear in Joyce criticism.

D129   Mercier, Vivian
"Joyce and the Irish Tradition of Parody", THE IRISH COMIC TRADITION (Oxford: Clarendon Press, 1962), pp. 210–36

Treats the comic elements of the Irish mentality and applies them to Joyce. This is an informed study that offers excellent background for an understanding of an important Irish tradition that Joyce worked against as well as from.

D130   Kumar, Shiv K.
"James Joyce", BERGSON AND THE STREAM OF CONSCIOUSNESS NOVEL (New York: New York University Press, 1963), pp. 103–38

Treats the parallels between Bergson's philosophical ideas and Joyce's technique.

D131   Stewart, J. I. M.
"Joyce", EIGHT MODERN WRITERS (Oxford: Clarendon Press, 1963), pp. 422–83

Based on his earlier National Book League pamphlet *James Joyce* (1957), this is an uncomfortable sixty-two page chapter which is appallingly narrow in its appraisal of Joyce's work and so constricted in its critical vision of *Finnegans Wake* that Stewart must frequently rely on Edmund Wilson's critical judgements written prior to 1931.

D132   Walzl, Florence L.
"The Liturgy of the Epiphany Season and the Epiphanies of Joyce", *PMLA*, 80:4 (September 1965), 436–450

An insightful piece that deals especially well with this important aspect of Joyce's early work.

D133   Hart, Clive
"James Joyce's Sentimentality", *Philological Quarterly*, 46 (1967), 516–26

Addresses the issue of sentimentality in Joyce's work, suggesting that his sentimental treatment of materials is a conspicuous attitude that indicates Joyce, much like Dickens and Lawrence, "seems unable to make an accurate assessment of the emotional potential of a subject". Uncertainty characterizes Joyce's sentimentality, though he constantly strives for a balanced point of view.

D134   Trilling, Lionel
"James Joyce in His Letters", *Commentary*, 45 (February 1968), 53–64

The first extended essay in response to the three published volumes of Joyce's letters. Although the immediate occasion for this essay was the publication of Joyce's letters, Trilling's comments on Joyce and his art go far beyond the letters themselves to explore Joyce's vision of man. He sees in all of Joyce's work a quality of disengagement and quiet nihilism. (Reprinted in D54.)

D135   Staley, Harry C.
"Joyce's Cathechisms", *James Joyce Quarterly*, 6:2 (Winter 1969), 137–53

A close examination of the influences of the Deharbe and Maynooth cathechisms on Joyce's ideas and style.

D136   Beja, Morris
        "James Joyce: The Bread of Everyday Life", EPIPHANY IN
        THE MODERN NOVEL (Seattle: University of Washington
        Press, 1971), pp. 71–111

        Within a book that studies the conception and function of the
        epiphany in a number of modern writers, Beja's discussion of
        Joyce's use of the epiphany is especially valuable.

D137   Poirier, Richard
        "The Literature of Waste: Eliot, Joyce, and Others", THE
        PERFORMING SELF (New York: Oxford University Press,
        1971), pp. 45–61

        Although brief comments, they are of value because they
        reflect a sensitive critic's understanding of Joyce's view of the
        world—a view Poirier believes Joyce shared with Eliot. The
        context observed here for Joyce's modernism is of interest.

D138   Flanagan, Thomas
        "Yeats, Joyce, and the Matter of Ireland", *Critical Inquiry*, 2
        (1975), 43–67

        Compares Joyce and Yeats in terms of their "Irish identity".

D139   Anderson, Chester G.
        "James Joyce as Sunny Jim: A Tale of a Tub", *James Joyce
        Quarterly*, 13:3 (Spring 1976), 328–49

        Explores the possible source of Joyce's nickname "Sunny Jim"
        in a jump-rope rhyme, an aetiology that leads Anderson to
        speculate in Freudian terms over Joyce's childhood copro-
        philic fantasies.

D140   O'Brien, Darcy
        "A Critique of Psychoanalytic Criticism, Or What Joyce Did
        and Did Not Do", *James Joyce Quarterly*, 13:3 (Spring
        1976), 275–92

        A cautionary view of psychoanalytic criticism generally and of
        James Joyce in particular. Especially interesting in light of
        O'Brien's earlier study of Joyce, *The Conscience of James
        Joyce* (1967).

D141   Spiegel, Alan
       FICTION AND THE CAMERA EYE: VISUAL
       CONSCIOUSNESS IN FILM AND THE MODERN
       NOVEL (Charlottesville: University Press of Virginia, 1976),
       pp. 63–8, 71–82, 90–7, 109–15, 136–50, 164–74

       An interesting and informed study of Joyce's cinematographic
       form in his fiction.

D142   Lodge, David
       "James Joyce", MODES OF MODERN WRITING:
       METAPHOR, METONOMY, AND THE TYPOLOGY OF
       MODERN LITERATURE (London: Arnold, 1977; Ithaca:
       Cornell University Press, 1977), pp. 125–44

       Discusses Joyce's early work as a transition between Roman
       Jakobson's metaphoric and metonymic poles, between the
       realistic and modernist texts. Lodge's work is especially
       interesting in its application of a linguistic model to Joyce's
       texts since most such studies of Joyce's work in the past have
       been devoted to *Finnegans Wake* and Lodge discusses Joyce's
       earlier works in this context.

D143   Benstock, Shari
       "The Dynamics of Narrative Performance: Stephen Dedalus
       as Storyteller", *ELH,* 49:3 (Fall 1982), 707–38

       A convincing theory of characterization in Joyce's work,
       based on defining characters as a matter of the stories they tell
       rather than the actions they commit. Thus what matters in the
       reading of Joyce's characters is how they transform the real
       events of their lives into narrative accounts that follow the
       age-old communal event of storytelling. The essay proceeds to
       describe the process of motivation by which such stories are
       produced in *Ulysses.*

D144   Deane, Seamus
       "Joyce and Nationalism", JAMES JOYCE: NEW
       PERSPECTIVES, ed. Colin MacCabe (Brighton, England:
       Harvester Press, 1982; Bloomington: Indiana University
       Press, 1982), pp. 168–183

       Explores the possible connection between the principles of

Joyce's art and political imagination. Deane's thesis is that although Joyce cannot be associated with a simple dialectic of politics, his art follows the same impulse as political rhetoric to give fictive aspirations an actual existence. Deane also notes that Joyce shares with Irish nationalism this faith in the transforming power of words. Even though no specific connection can be made, service to art, in Joyce's case, was also service to Ireland.

D145   Splitter, Randolph
        "Watery Words: Language, Sexuality, and Motherhood in Joyce's Fiction", *ELH*, 49:1 (Spring 1982), 190–213

Offers brief deconstructive readings of the major works in terms of Joyce's preoccupation with language and infantile fantasies. One distinctive facet of Splitter's analysis is his contention that *Finnegans Wake* mediates between a literalness of language and a metaphoricity of relations between things, thus forming a text that is at once logocentric and deconstructive. Given the importance of deconstruction in recent Joyce studies, this essay provides a well-conceived application.

D146   Schenker, Daniel
        "Stalking the Invisible Hero: Ibsen, Joyce, Kierkegaard, and the Failure of Modern Irony", *ELH*, 51:1 (Spring 1984), 153–83

Traces Joyce's predilection for the bourgeois hero over the larger-than-life hero of traditional fiction, a notion Joyce derived from Ibsen. In this light, Stephen appears as a false hero because he strives for an extraordinary art, yet it is a striving even Stephen looks upon with ironic distance. Bloom, however, because he is the most ordinary, is the most heroic of Joyce's characters and also bears affinity to Kierkegaard's interpretation of Abraham.

Special Issues

D147   "Homage to James Joyce", *transition*, 21 (1932), 245–82

Consists mainly of tributes paid Joyce on his fiftieth birthday and tenth anniversary of the publication of *Ulysses*. Of special interest is the translation of "Anna Livia Plurabelle" into everyday English. Also included are an appreciative essay on "Work in Progress" by Louis Gillet which first appeared in the prestigious *Revue des Deux Mondes*, and Joyce's own translation into French of a short poem by James Stevens. Another item of interest is a whimsical, irreverent and anonymous essay which pokes fun at Stuart Gilbert and Joyce's classical learning, and concludes with a tribute to Oliver St John Gogarty, the Dublin personality upon whom the character of Buck Mulligan is based.

D148   "Special Joyce Issue", *Envoy*, 5 (May 1951), 6–78

A diverse group of essays and reminiscences by Irish contributors. Some pieces such as the ones by Andrew Cass and Niall Montgomery are harshly critical of Joyce. Another essay by Patrick Kavanagh complains of the academizing of Joyce, especially by American scholars. Further items of interest are the classical scholar W. B. Stanford's essay on the Homeric parallel and Joseph Hone's recollection of considering *Dubliners* for publication, when he worked for Maunsel and Company, and why the manuscript was rejected. This collection, edited by the Irish writer Brian Nolan (Flann O'Brien), offers a clear view of the contradictory responses Joyce continues to elicit from his countrymen.

D149   "James Joyce Special Number", *Modern Fiction Studies*, 4 (1958), 3–99

Contains eight original essays, many of which explore the early work of Joyce and provide a defence of the character of Stephen Dedalus. A. Walton Litz provides a general discussion of the *Ulysses* notesheets for "Cyclops" through "Penelope". Grant Redford discusses *A Portrait* in terms of how the book's themes are reflected in the structure. Julian B. Kaye writes, in a defence of *Dubliners*, that these stories have the same richness of texture as *Ulysses* or *Finnegans Wake* and claims that Joyce was at the height of his powers when he wrote "The Dead". D. J. F. Aitken focuses on *Exiles* and how the character of Richard can be associated with Joyce's familiar symbols such as the moon goddess and earth elements. Robert Bierman discusses the language of *Finnegans Wake* and makes an argument for the value of its unintelligibility. This *MFS* issue, which includes discussion of the Dedalus controversy, provides a response to the "Stephen Hating School" attributed to Hugh Kenner.

D150   "Translation Issue", *James Joyce Quarterly*, 4:3 (Spring 1967), 163–246

Edited by Fritz Senn, the essays deal with various aspects and problems relating to the translation of Joyce. Senn's essay, "Seven Against *Ulysses*", which refers to the seven translations of *Ulysses* he treats, has been frequently reprinted in expanded versions. In addition to other essays and notes, this issue contains specimen passages of translations in progress.

D151   "James Joyce Special Number", *Modern Fiction Studies*, 15 (1969), 3–182

This special issue is devoted to a broad variety of topics. Bernard Benstock traces allegorical and anagogical superstructures in *Finnegans Wake*, emphasising sexual guilt. John White speculates on the metaphysical growth of Joyce seen in the evolving creative vision of *Ulysses*. Ralph Jenkins explores the metaphysical dimension of stability and instability in "Scylla and Charybdis". Phillip Herring deals with Joyce's preoccupation with marital infidelity. An essay by William Jenkins draws a connection between A. Conan Doyle and Joyce. Of special importance is the selected but substantial checklist on Joyce criticism through 1968.

D152   Zyla, Wolodymyr T., ed.
JAMES JOYCE: HIS PLACE IN WORLD LITERATURE:
PROCEEDINGS OF THE COMPARATIVE
LITERATURE SYMPOSIUM, II, FEBRUARY 7 AND 8
1969 (Lubbock: Interdepartmental Committee on
Comparative Literature, Texas Technical College, 1969)

Six original papers presented at a comparative literature conference which have as their general theme Joyce's contribution to literature outside of the English-speaking countries.

D153 "James Joyce in the Seventies: The Expanding Dimensions of His Art", *Studies in the Literary Imagination*, 3:2 (1970), 1–96

A rather bland collection of essays that attempts to give a contemporary view of Joyce scholarship.

D154 "A James Joyce Number", *Dublin Magazine*, 10:2 (1973), 21–32; 42–76; 106–12

Bernard Benstock writes on the Swiftian inheritance as it applies to Joyce's early journalistic essays and the poem "The Holy Office"; Richard Kain comments on the importance of geographical locale to the Irish artist; John Ryan reveals maritime documents that prove the *Rosevean*, a ship mentioned in *Ulysses*, was an actual vessel; American elements in "An Encounter" are explored by Sam Bluefarb; and John Raymond Hart examines the influence of George Moore's *The Untilled Field* on Joyce.

D155 "Joyce and Modern Psychology", *James Joyce Quarterly*, 13:3 (1976), 266–384

This issue contains essays that apply psychoanalytic theory to Joyce's life and writing. With the exception of Darcy O'Brien's general criticism of depth psychology, they reflect the view that psychoanalysis is the best tool we have for exploring psychic motives in literature. Included is Mark Shechner's firm defence of depth psychology as a reading method. This issue also contains a selected bibliography of Joyce and psychoanalysis.

D156 Aubert, Jacques, and Maria Jolas, eds
Joyce & Paris: 1902 ... 1920–1940 ... 1975. PAPERS FROM THE 5TH INTERNATIONAL JAMES JOYCE SYMPOSIUM, PARIS 16–20 JUNE 1975, 2 vols (Paris: Editions du CNRS, 1979)

Records papers, panels and other material relating to the Paris symposium, a congress of Joyce scholars that was given added importance by the participation of Maria Jolas, one of Joyce's closest friends. The first volume, entirely in French, contains the lecture by the neo-Freudian psychoanalyst and philosopher Jacques Lacan. Included in the second volume are tape transcriptions of lectures and panel sessions in English, such as Morris Beja's on political perspectives in Joyce's work. This panel developed into an intense and sometimes heated discussion over a controversial issue. Other symposium participants whose contributions are recorded include Richard Ellmann, Leslie Fiedler and Michel Butor.

D157   "Structuralist/Reader Response Issue", *James Joyce Quarterly*, 16:1-2 (Fall 1978-Winter 1979), 5-149

New critical methodologies are treated in this issue: deconstruction, structuralism, and reader response. Included is a publishing history of *Tel Quel*, a journal which encapsulates much of the French contribution to Joycean critical analysis. Robert Scholes, David Hayman and Joseph Kestner contribute articles on structuralism; reader-response approaches are contributed by Brook Thomas and Fritz Senn. These essays serve to open up the question of textuality, and more specifically of narrative, in ways which reflect recent developments in literary theory.

D158   "Special James Joyce Combined Volume", *Modern British Literature*, 5 (1980), 1-79

A special two-number Joyce issue of *Modern British Literature* contains nine essays by such critics as Fritz Senn, Bernard Benstock, Thomas F. Staley and Zack Bowen. It also includes Joseph Kestner, "Joyce, Wagner and Bizet: *Exiles, Tannhauser,* and *Carmen*"; Michael Groden, "James Joyce and the Classical, Romantic, and Modern Tempers"; and Brook Thomas, "Reading, Writing, and Joyce's Dublin".

D159   "The Murge Project: 'Araby' as Story and Discourse", *James Joyce Quarterly* 18:3 (Spring 1981), 237-99

A full-scale analysis of "Araby" based on Seymour Chatman's discussion of narration, point of view, setting and character (from *Story and Discourse*). The articles contained in this issue include a sentence-by-sentence narratological description of "Araby" as well as a critical dialogue between Chatman, Jonathan Culler and Gerald Prince regarding lack of agreement over how Chatman's theory should be applied.

D160 IRISH RENAISSANCE ANNUAL II (Newark: University of Delaware Press, 1981)

A collection of essays on various themes in *Dubliners, A Portrait* and *Ulysses*. John Henry Raleigh is featured in the Annual with an essay of substantial length that fits the Eumaeus chapter into a political and historical context. Deborah Mantell explores the contemporary Irish national character and Joyce's position on Irish political history in the light of Leopold Bloom. James Carens and Margaret Church consider sexual perceptions in *A Portrait*, the former dealing with the motif of hands, the latter with Stephen's adolescent views of women. Thomas Connolly applies Stephen's aesthetic theory to the structure of *A Portrait*, providing reinterpretations of former criticism and new insight into the structural rhythm of the novel. J. F. Lyons, a Dublin physician, looks at the pattern of physical afflictions in *Dubliners'* characters, especially alcoholism, as a part of the general theme of paralysis.

D161 "Studies in the Early Joyce", *Cahiers Victoriens & Édouardiens*, 14 (October 1981), 1–121

A collection of essays, three of them in English, devoted to the early writings of Joyce. Included are analyses of individual *Dubliners* stories, the epiphanies, and aspects of *Ulysses*. Most pieces are by French critics, although there is an essay on Gogarty and Joyce by Fritz Senn.

D162 "James Joyce (1882–1941)", *Scripsi*, 2:1 (November 1982), 1–137

A centenary collection of essays by well-established Joyce critics. In many of the essays (Empson, Fiedler, D. J. O'Hearn) Hugh Kenner is a target for less than convincing reproaches. Some pieces are characterized by a directness, even vulgarity (Peter Craven on *Ulysses*), and most (excepting Senn) show casual regard for the convention of the footnote. Yet, these essays, despite sometimes crude scholarship and expression, contain an impressive array of polemics, playfulness, and perception.

D163   "James Joyce and the Arts in Ireland", *The Crane Bag*, 6:1
        (Dublin 1982)

An issue which includes many Irish contributors commemorat-
ing the Joyce centenary. Sheldon Brivic offers a psychological
appreciation of Joyce's creative process. Mark Patrick
Hederman considers Joyce as both poet and priest in a survey
of the major works. Gerald Y. Goldberg, Dublin lawyer and
litterateur, writes on the Jewish dimension of Joyce's art.

D164   "James Joyce and His Contemporaries", *Comparative
        Literature Studies*, 19 (Summer 1982), 97–279

This special issue, edited by Bernard Benstock, contains eleven
essays which reflect contemporary critical concerns and their
relation to Joyce's work. Among these essays are four which
touch upon Joyce's impact on Latin American literature. Also
offers essays on Joyce, Picasso and Britten as caricaturists, on
Mauthner's *Critique of Language* and its influence on
Finnegans Wake, on Jung and *Ulysses*, and on noise and
rumour in *Finnegans Wake*, among others. As Benstock notes
in his introduction, "the essays in this collection are as eclectic
as any editor could have hoped for."

D165   "The James Joyce Centenary", *Renascence*, 35:2 (Winter
        1983)

A special issue dedicated to Robert R. Boyle. Hugh Kenner
speculates on the influence of Joyce's teaching of basic English
to foreigners upon his writing; Thomas F. Staley explores the
connection between Joyce and Edouard Dujardin; Mary
Reynolds draws a parallel between apostate Joyce and the
French religious iconoclast Renan; Florence Walzl distinguishes fact from fiction in "Clay"; Michael Patrick Gillespie
charts Catholic precepts and iconography in Chapter 7 of
Finnegans Wake.

Poetry and Minor Works

See also: D32, D85 and D98

E1   Tindall, William York

"Introduction", "The Texts of Chamber Music", and "Notes to the Poems", JAMES JOYCE'S *CHAMBER MUSIC*, ed. Tindall (New York: Columbia University Press, 1954), pp. 3–98, 98–106, and 181–225

The most extended critical commentary on the poetry is offered in the introduction and notes to this edition. Although Tindall gives much useful biographical and source material, his scatological interpretation of the poems has been quite properly rejected by most Joyce critics.

E2   Baker, James R.
"Joyce's *Chamber Music*: The Exile of the Heart", *Arizona Quarterly*, 15 (Winter 1959), 349–356

Offers a broad thematic reading of the sequence stressing the exile.

E3   Scholes, Robert
"James Joyce, Irish Poet", *James Joyce Quarterly*, 2 (Summer 1965), 255–270

An interesting discussion of Joyce as an Irish poet whose poetry should be looked at in light of the humanists' conception of poetry.

E4   Bowen, Zack
"Goldenhair: Joyce's Archetypal Female", *Literature and Psychology*, 17 (1967), 219–28

Traces Joyce's archetypal nine figure throughout the poems and relates it to the women in the later works.

E5   Staley, Thomas F.
"The Poet Joyce and the Shadow of Swift", JONATHAN
SWIFT: TERCENTENARY ESSAYS, eds Winston
Weathers and Thomas F. Staley, Monograph Series, 3 (Tulsa,
Okla.: University of Tulsa, 1967), pp. 39–52

Looks at Swiftian attitudes and qualities in two of Joyce's
satiric poems.

E6   Von Phul, Ruth
"*Chamber Music* at the *Wake*", *James Joyce Quarterly*, 11:4
(Summer 1974), 355–67

A Freudian analysis of the poems through the looking-glass of
Finnegans Wake.

E7   Russel, Myra
"The Elizabethan Connection: The Missing Score of James
Joyce's *Chamber Music*", *James Joyce Quarterly*, 18:2
(Winter 1981), 133–146

Following a brief description of the relationship between
poetry and music in Elizabethan England, the author traces
connecting links between *Chamber Music* and the lyric
conventions of the earlier age.

Dubliners

Most of the cross-listings below refer to the general works that devote chapters or large sections to *Dubliners*; they provide commentary on *Dubliners* as a whole or contain analyses of individual stories.
See also: D4, D6, D8, D10, D12, D19, D23, D28, D30, D31, D32, D45, D46, D64, D72, D77, D88, D98, D142, D159, D165, G10 and G12.

Books

F1   Gifford, Don
       JOYCE ANNOTATED-NOTES FOR *DUBLINERS* AND
       A PORTRAIT OF THE ARTIST AS A YOUNG MAN
       (1967; 2nd edn, Berkeley, Los Angeles and London:
       University of California Press, 1982)

       An indispensable reference work which provides not only key explanations of Dublin vocabulary and textual allusions but also introductory sections on matters such as monetary values in the story "Eveline". The revised version (which replaces the previous edition) has maps which document locales in *Dubliners* and corrects a number of earlier mistakes.

F2   Garrett, Peter K., ed.
       TWENTIETH CENTURY INTERPRETATIONS OF
       DUBLINERS: A COLLECTION OF CRITICAL ESSAYS
       (Englewood Cliffs, N.J.: Prentice Hall, 1968)

       Garrett's introductory essay to this collection stresses the major points of Joyce's artistry in *Dubliners*: indirect style, epiphany, symbolism, objective depiction, thematic content and structural unity. These aspects are taken up in essays by such noted Joyce scholars as Robert Boyle, S. L. Goldberg, Hugh Kenner and Florence Walzl. The volume touches on each of the stories from *Dubliners*. All of these essays appeared previously in journals.

F3   Baker, James R., and Thomas F. Staley, eds
       JAMES JOYCE'S *DUBLINERS*: A CRITICAL
       HANDBOOK (Belmont, California: Wadsworth, 1969)

Offers a selection of previously published essays on the stories by various critics as well as an extensive but now dated bibliography.

F4   Beck, Warren
JOYCE'S *DUBLINERS*: SUBSTANCE, VISION AND ART (Durham, N.C.: Duke University Press, 1969)

Beck's study reveals a blissful ignorance of all previous interpretations and at the same time assumes a rather dogmatic and lofty posture in his own analysis. Nevertheless, his book is not without insight. He frequently renders a careful and sensitive reading of individual stories, but his is a work that is lacking in the necessary dialogue of scholarship.

F5   Hart, Clive, ed.
JAMES JOYCE'S *DUBLINERS*: CRITICAL ESSAYS (London: Faber and Faber, 1969; New York: Viking, 1969)

A collection of original critical essays, each covering one of the *Dubliners* stories. The fifteen different contributors, with two or three exceptions, have provided sound readings of the stories that illustrate their individual richness and complexity and the wide variety of approaches they elicit. John William Carrington comments on how the priest and the young boy in "The Sisters" exchange identities; Fritz Senn explores the naturalistic setting and the spirit of unruliness which pervades all characters in "Encounter"; J. S. Atherton examines the theory that every detail in "Araby" contributes to the total effect; Clive Hart looks at how choices of detail and diction in "Eveline" support the general theme of paralysis versus change; Zack Bowen considers the image pattern in "After the Race" and how it reflects thematic development; "Two Gallants" is described by A. Walton Litz as inverting the stock expectations of gallantry and romantic fiction; Nathan Halper looks at Homeric parallels in "A Boarding House" and speculates on autobiographical aspects in the character of Bob Doran; Robert Boyle sees Chandler in "A Little Cloud" as Joyce's version of a Dublin artist, a trapped frustrated dreamer; Robert Scholes develops the concept of "counterparts" both in the story by that title and in *Dubliners* as a whole; Adaline Glasheen offers a sensitive and highly sympathetic sketch of the plight of Maria in "Clay"; Thomas Connolly speculates on how Mr Duffy in "A Painful Case" is both protagonist and antagonist, reflecting in his divided character the aspects of Stanislaus and James Joyce; M. J. C. Hodgart concentrates on the figure of Parnell and Irish politics in "Ivy Day in the Committee Room"; shifting points of narration is the subject of David Hayman's essay on "A Mother"; Richard Kain comments on how tone brings out an atmosphere of feigned gentility and pomposity in "Grace" and how Joyce used the story as a preparation for *Ulysses*; and Bernard Benstock offers summary analysis not only of "The Dead" but of *Dubliners*, noting that Joyce's final story is his ironic tale of Epiphany Day, a statement on the decay of Irish Christianity to a state of self-mockery. As this volume evidences, scholarship on *Dubliners* has borne out the work's intricate and seminal relationship to Joyce's mature art, as well as its own aesthetic importance. This book helped establish a trend in criticism of *Dubliners* toward looking even more closely at its pivotal position in the development of Joyce's canon.

F6   Scholes, Robert, and A. Walton Litz, eds
       DUBLINERS: TEXT, CRITICISM AND NOTES (New York: Viking, 1969)

       Includes a number of essays and some background materials as well as selected bibliography and notes on the stories which summarize and stress the importance of *Dubliners* in the Joyce canon. Noting the life stages in the structure, the editors emphasize that "the real hero of the stories is not an individual but the city itself, a city whose geography, history and inhabitants are all part of a coherent vision; and in this aspect *Dubliners* anticipates the anatomy of the modern city made by Joyce in *Ulysses*. Even *Finnegans Wake*, with its fabric of rumour and 'popular' culture, may be seen as an extension of the world of *Dubliners*."

F7   Reichert, Klaus, Fritz Senn and Dieter F. Zimmer, eds
       MATERIALIEN ZU JAMES JOYCE *DUBLINERS* (Frankfurt-am-Main: Suhrkamp, 1969)

       An excellent volume which provides charted maps of Dublin tracing the journeys of the characters in the various stories.

F8   San Juan, Epifanio, Jr
       JAMES JOYCE AND THE CRAFT OF FICTION: AN

INTERPRETATION OF *DUBLINERS* (Rutherford, N.J.: Fairleigh Dickinson University Press, 1972)

San Juan spends a great deal of time attacking earlier interpretations and then renders rather narrow moral readings of the characters and offers some untenable conclusions which attempt to find humble virtues in nearly all the characters.

F9   Beja, Morris
JAMES JOYCE: *DUBLINERS* and *A PORTRAIT OF THE ARTIST AS A YOUNG MAN:* A CASEBOOK (London: Macmillan, 1973)

Includes such essays on *Dubliners* as Richard Ellmann's on the biographical background of "The Dead", Brewster Ghiselin's early but important analysis of the unity in *Dubliners*, and Anthony Burgess' piece on the theme of paralysis. This collection also offers early reviews of *Dubliners*.

F10   Scholes, Robert
SEMIOTIC APPROACHES TO A FICTIONAL TEXT: JOYCE'S "EVELINE", (Moscow: University of Idaho, 1976); also published in *James Joyce Quarterly*, 16:1–2 (Fall–Winter 1979), 65–80

A monograph which shows how the theoretical models of Todorov, Genette, and Barthes, each approach developed for a particular text, can be combined in a manner that has potential for "the practical criticism" of a broader range of texts. This is a valuable essay in its forecasting of future possibilities and trends in Joyce criticism.

F11   Bidwell, Bruce, and Linda Heffer
THE JOYCEAN WAY. A TOPOGRAPHIC GUIDE TO *DUBLINERS* AND *A PORTRAIT OF THE ARTIST AS A YOUNG MAN* (Baltimore: Johns Hopkins University Press, 1982)

Based on the obvious insight that topographic details are important to the Joyce text. Despite numerous errors, the authors attempt to do for early Joyce fiction what Hart and Knuth have done for *Ulysses* and Louis O. Mink for

Finnegans Wake. Photographs, maps, and biographical details provide a tour of actual sites in *Dubliners* and *A Portrait* (including historical and mythical details). The most valuable part of this book is the glossary and index of place names, an accurate topographical guide of the Dublin environs.

F12   Torchiana, Donald T.
       BACKGROUNDS FOR JOYCE'S *DUBLINERS* (Boston: Allen & Unwin, 1986)

Surveys critical scholarship on *Dubliners* and focuses upon the backgrounds to each story rather than interpretation. Torchiana discusses elements of Joyce's stories which might be missed by the reader unfamiliar with Irish legend, place-names, nationalism, myth and religious divisions. But his discussion, however interesting, frequently strays from a close context with the story at hand. A substantial portion of the book is devoted to analysing previous critical responses to *Dubliners*, but Torchiana spends too much time attacking some critics for their shortcomings and occasionally forcing his hypothesis that the stories are actually a "series of mirror-images" which correspond almost exclusively to real correlatives.

Articles and Chapters in Books

F13   Pound, Ezra
       "*Dubliners* and Mr James Joyce", *Egoist*, 1 (1914), 267

Pound's early insightful review of *Dubliners* which emphasizes Joyce's carefully restrained style of selective detail based on the realism of Flaubert. This article has been widely reprinted but the above citation notes its first appearance. (Reprinted in B27 and D108.)

F14   Levin, Richard, and Charles Shattuck
       "First Flight to Ithaca: A New Reading of Joyce's *Dubliners*", *Accent*, 4 (1944), 75–99

A daring interpretation of *Dubliners* which applies the Homeric parallel of the *Odyssey* to the individual stories. This is an oversimplified and Procrustean reading, but it did focus attention on the unity of the work and prompted later critics to look more carefully at this aspect. (Reprinted in D6.)

F15   Tate, Allen
"Three Commentaries", *Sewanee Review*, 58 (1950), 1–15

Tate was one of the earliest critics to point out Joyce's method of using naturalistic details to achieve symbolic meaning, a subject that has received a good deal of subsequent attention in relation to all of the stories.

F16   Noon, William T., S. J.
"Joyce's 'Clay': An Interpretation", *College English*, 17 (1955), 93–95

An attempt to explain "Clay" in its relationship to All Hallows Eve with focus falling on Maria.

F17   Ghiselin, Brewster
"The Unity of Joyce's *Dubliners*", *Accent*, 16 (1956), 75–88; 196–231

An early and influential study that stresses the unity and remains one of the most extensive analyses of the structure of *Dubliners*. He argues that the collection is not loose and episodic but "really unitary", asserting that a symbolic structure is given to *Dubliners* through significantly disposed controlling images and metaphors which function throughout to make *Dubliners* a sustained and unified work of art. While many of his specific interpretations seem forced, Ghiselin's general view still holds much critical weight. (Reprinted in F2, F3, F6 and F9.)

F18   Ostroff, Anthony
"The Moral Vision in *Dubliners*", *Western Speech*, 20 (1956), 196–209

Argues that the essential unity is an aesthetic, not a thematic, design; that this unity is afforded by a consistency of vision; and that this "moral vision is the reality behind the stories." Ostroff's thesis with its emphasis on unity of theme sets the tone for a great deal of the future criticism of *Dubliners*.

F19   O'Hehir, Brendan
        "Structural Symbol in Joyce's 'The Dead'", *Twentieth Century Literature*, 3 (1957), 3–13

        Looks at the symbolic significance of such naturalistic details as Gabriel's galoshes and his speech mannerisms and shows how they heighten the portrayal of Gabriel's alienation from Dublin culture.

F20   Carpenter, Richard, and Daniel Leary
        "The Witch Maria", *James Joyce Review,* 3 (1959), 3–7

        Traces clearly the witchlike overtones of Maria in "Clay". The authors suggest that Maria is a bringer of discord to the ones she most loves, but it is an unintentional destructiveness. To read Maria as a witch also requires one to ignore several incidents where she prevents discord, but, more importantly, such a reading ignores the ironic dimensions of this complex story. This essay is an example of the many extreme interpretations of *Dubliners* stories that were written in the fifties.

F21   Walzl, Florence L.
        "Pattern of Paralysis in Joyce's *Dubliners:* A Study of the Original Framework", *College English,* 22 (1961), 221–28

        Stresses Joyce's therapeutic bent of mind as he analysed the social illness of Dublin and structured the paralytic condition of its inhabitants into stories that conclude with an even greater note of paralysis.

F22   Baker, James R.
        "Ibsen, Joyce, and the Living-Dead: A Story of *Dubliners*", A JAMES JOYCE MISCELLANY, THIRD SERIES, ed. Marvin Magalaner (Carbondale: Southern Illinois University Press, 1962), pp. 19–32

        Points out Joyce's debt to Ibsen in which he adopted Ibsen's basic metaphor of the paralysed life to describe those who are living but spiritually dead. (Reprinted in F3.)

F23   Walzl, Florence L.
        "Joyce's 'Clay': Fact and Fiction", *Explicator*, 20 (February
        1962), Item 46

        Concentrates on the ambiguous and contradictory elements of
        the setting and character of Maria. In order to stress the
        realism of the story, Walzl makes use of public records to
        establish the exact position of an institutional matron upon
        which Maria's character is based. (Reprinted in F2.)

F24   Boyle, Robert, S. J.
        "'Two Gallants' and 'Ivy Day in the Committee Room'",
        James Joyce Quarterly, 1:1 (Fall 1963), 3–9

        Interpretation based on symbolic meanings. Corley and
        Lenehan, in "Two Gallants", represent the figures of knight
        and squire respectively. In "Ivy Day", the impact of Hynes'
        poem is considered as stronger than the forces of political
        betrayal and despair. A good example of the close readings of
        the individual stories that appeared throughout the fifties and
        sixties. (Reprinted in F2.)

F25   O'Connor, Frank
        "Work in Progress", THE LONELY VOICE: A STUDY OF
        THE SHORT STORY (Cleveland: World, 1963), pp. 113–27

        Traces how Joyce necessarily abandoned the short story in
        order to take advantage of the stylistic and structural
        expansiveness of the novel form. Includes speculation on the
        lost manuscript of "Mr Hunter's Day", a story originally
        planned for *Dubliners* but eventually to become the kernel
        plot for *Ulysses*. (Reprinted in F2 and F6.)

F26   Hagopian, John V.
        "'Counterparts'", INSIGHT II: ANALYSES OF MODERN
        BRITISH LITERATURE, ed. Hagopian and Martin Dolch
        (Frankfurt, Germany: Hirschgraben, 1964), pp. 201–6

        A resourceful interpretation of "Counterparts" as an epiphany
        of the sin of anger. During the sixties many of the *Dubliners*
        stories were interpreted in light of Joyce's comments on the
        "epiphany" as a literary device. (Reprinted in F3.)

F27   Stein, William B.
"'Counterparts': A Swine Song", *James Joyce Quarterly*, 1:2 (Winter 1964), 30–2

Explores animality and vice in the character of Farrington against a backdrop of a Catholic calendar. Compares "Counterparts" and Joyce's use of similar qualities in characters such as Maria and Father Flynn from other stories.

F28   Carrier, Warren
"*Dubliners*: Joyce's Dantean Vision", *Renascence*, 17 (1965), 211–215

Concentrates on the three key words in the opening story—paralysis, simony, and gnomon—as key thematic and stylistic indicators of the entire work. These three words are then interpreted in terms of Dantean psychology and theology.

F29   Connolly, Thomas E.
"Joyce's 'The Sisters': A Pennyworth of Snuff", *College English*, 27 (1965), 189–95

Returns to a simple reading of "The Sisters" to counter what Connolly considers wild, speculative interpretations such as the issue of whether Father Flynn has committed an act of simony. The theme of the story is treated as simple and straightforward: a young boy's acceptance of a friend's death. (Reprinted in F3.)

F30   Feshbach, Sidney
"Death in 'An Encounter'", *James Joyce Quarterly*, 2:2 (Winter 1965), 82–9

Treats the story as an elegiac form which laments and finally transcends the spiritual death of the young boy narrator.

F31   Friedrich, Gerhard
"The Perspective of Joyce's *Dubliners*", *College English*, 24 (1965), 421–6

Examines each story in terms of theme and symbolism. (Reprinted in F3.)

F32   Kelleher, John V.
"Irish History and Mythology in James Joyce's 'The Dead'",
Review of Politics, 27 (1965), 414–33

An illuminating source study which also suggests the way in
which Joyce used Irish myth and history for dramatic and
ironic effect. An important essay for its recognition of the
depth and complexity of Joyce's early art.

F33   Niemeyer, Carl
"'Grace' and Joyce's Method of Parody", *College English*, 27
(1965), 196–201

Looks at "Grace" as a parody of Dante's *Divine Comedy*, a
parody that yet retains moral significance as a portrayal of
Dublin's debased condition. (Reprinted in F3.)

F34   Senn, Fritz
"'He Was Too Scrupulous Always': Joyce's 'The Sisters'",
James Joyce Quarterly, 2:2 (Winter 1965), 66–72

An act of attention to single words and phrases, drawing much
allusive complexity from Joyce's verbal play in "The Sisters".

F35   Smith, Thomas F.
"Color and Light in 'The Dead'", *James Joyce Quarterly*, 2:4
(Summer 1965), 304–9

An example of symbolic interpretation that dominated the
reading of this story through the fifties and sixties.

F36   Stone, Harry
"'Araby' and the Writings of James Joyce", *Antioch Review*,
25 (1965), 375–410

A long and detailed essay that begins with "Araby" as an
autobiographical focus for Joyce. After close analysis of the
story's plot, Stone speculates on the crucial experience of
youthful disillusionment as it appears in Joyce's later writings.

F37   Walzl, Florence L.
"Ambiguity in the Structural Symbols of Gabriel's Vision in

Joyce's 'The Dead'", *Wisconsin Studies in English*, 2
(Madison: Wisconsin Teachers of English, 1965)

One of Walzl's early studies which concentrates on the
structural principles which give aesthetic dimension to Joyce.
Walzl explores the ambiguity of the final epiphany of Gabriel
in "The Dead", demonstrating that the ambiguity is not only
deliberate but a summation of the "moral history" of
Dubliners.

F38   Walzl, Florence L.
"Symbolism in Joyce's 'Two Gallants'", *James Joyce
Quarterly*, 2:2 (Winter 1965), 73–81

Presents the interpretation that in addition to social and
political betrayal, there is a spiritual level of betrayal which is
an ironic parallel to the life of Christ on Holy Thursday.

F39   Connolly, Thomas E.
"Marriage Divination in Joyce's 'Clay'", *Studies in Short
Fiction*, 3 (1966), 293–9

Traces three distinct rituals of marriage divination in "Clay",
which provide both a structural and thematic integrity for the
story.

F40   Staley, Thomas F.
"Moral Responsibility in Joyce's 'Clay'", *Renascence*, 18
(1966), 124–8

Avoids symbolic interpretations of the story to concentrate on
the facts which illustrate Maria's epiphany of the utter lack of
moral responsibility in her world.

F41   Walzl, Florence L.
"Gabriel and Michael: The Conclusion of 'The Dead'",
James Joyce Quarterly 4:1 (Fall 1966), 17–31

Summarizes earlier interpretations of the ending and
concludes that the ambiguity is deliberate, for the story
gathers all of the earlier themes of *Dubliners* into a deeper and
more profound meaning. (Reprinted in F6.)

F42   apRoberts, Robert P.
"'Araby' and the Palimpsest of Criticism; or, through a Glass
Eye Darkly", *Antioch Review*, 26 (1966–7), 469–89

The immediate occasion for this essay was a rebuttal to Harry
Stone's article (F35) in the previous issue. The author attacks
Stone's symbolic reading and oversymbolic readings generally.
Quite interesting also because of its general points related to
interpretations of Joyce's fiction.

F43   Benstock, Bernard
"Arabesques: Third Position of Concord", *James Joyce
Quarterly*, 5:1 (Fall 1967), 30–9

Mediates the critical debate over "Araby" by critics Harry
Stone and Robert P. apRoberts (Fall 1965, Winter 1966–7
issues of *Antioch Review*), synthesizing what he believes to be
the strongest elements of both.

F44   Collins, Ben L.
"Joyce's 'Araby' and the 'Extended Simile'", *James Joyce
Quarterly*, 4:2 (Winter 1967), 84–90

Defines "Araby" with respect to a new literary term, the
"extended simile", a device which has not only a comparative
but a differentiating function on several levels of meaning that
affects an entire work. (Reprinted in F2.)

F45   Rosenberg, Bruce A.
"The Crucifixion in 'The Boarding House'", *Studies in Short
Fiction*, 5 (1967), 44–53

Avoids the usual reading of this story as the conflation of a
boarding house with a brothel, instead concentrating on the
religious significance of the naturalistic details.

F46   Trilling, Lionel
"Commentary", THE EXPERIENCE OF LITERATURE,
ed. Lionel Trilling (New York: Holt, 1967), pp. 652–5

Argues that "The Dead" ends on an ambiguous note resulting
from Joyce's own rising sympathy, a sympathy which

overcomes his earlier ironic tone in the story. (Reprinted in F3.)

F47   Scholes, Robert
        "A Commentary on 'Clay'", ELEMENTS OF FICTION
        (New York: Oxford University Press, 1968), pp. 66–77

        A lucid interpretation of basic story elements such as plot,
        character, tone, style and symbolism. Scholes stresses that
        Joyce's method of writing demands that a reader share in the
        construction of a story.

F48   Boyle, Robert, S. J.
        "Swiftian Allegory and Dantean Parody in Joyce's 'Grace'",
        James Joyce Quarterly, 7:1 (Fall 1969), 11–21

        Traces the parodic biblical overtones in "Grace" in terms of the
        various sects of Christianity.

F49   Chatman, Seymour
        "New Ways of Analyzing Narrative Structure with an
        example from Joyce's *Dubliners*", *Language and Style*, 2
        (1969), 3–36

        In part a combination of Roland Barthes and Tzvetan
        Todorov's theories of narrative structure in fiction. Taking the
        sentence as the basic unit of interpretation, Chatman reduces
        the story to a symbolic code, allowing him to chart precisely
        the logistics of plot and characterization.

F50   Easson, Angus
        "Parody as Comment in James Joyce's 'Clay'", *James Joyce
        Quarterly*, 7:2 (Winter 1970), 75–81

        Discusses the dual role of Maria as both naive optimist and as
        potentially perceptive realist, a double vision that is related to
        Joyce's technique. This essay reflects the sustained arguments
        and counterarguments over the interpretation of Maria in the
        story.

F51   Engel, Monroe
        "*Dubliners* and Erotic Expectations", TWENTIETH

CENTURY LITERATURE IN RETROSPECT, ed. Reuben
A. Brower (Cambridge, Mass.: Harvard University Press,
1971), pp. 3–26

Argues that the "conflict between high erotic aspiration and a
low estimate of the possibility of erotic fulfilment is very near
the dynamic center of Joyce's literary production". This
conflict is pervasive, according to Engel, and is revealed in
Joyce's use of irony.

F52   Fischer-Seidel, Therese
"From Reliable to Unreliable Narrator: Rhetorical Changes
in Joyce's 'The Sisters'", *James Joyce Quarterly*, 9:1 (Fall
1971), 85–92

Compares the early version of this story in the magazine *Irish
Homestead* to the final version as a basis for comments on
Joyce's developing power of narrative sophistication.

F53   Sloan, Barbara L.
"The D'Annunzian Narrator in 'A Painful Case': Silent,
Exiled and Cunning", *James Joyce Quarterly*, 9:1 (Fall 1971),
26–36

Analyses the character of Duffy in terms of Stephen Dedalus'
formula for "silence, cunning and exile", which is seen as
Joyce's version of the D'Annunzian concept of the poet
standing outside humanity.

F54   Solomon, Albert J.
"The Background of 'Eveline'", *Eire*, 6:3 (1971), 23–38

Like many essays on the individual stories this one traces the
historical and literary background, pointing out parallels with
two of George Moore's stories.

F55   Ormsby, Frank, and John Cronin
"'A Very Fine Piece of Writing': 'Ivy Day in the Committee
Room'", *Eire*, 7:1 (1972), 84–94

Attempts to avoid the "retrospective interpretation" of
Dubliners wherein the stories are read in terms of Joyce's later

work. This article offers a close reading of the text, drawing straightforward conclusions.

F56   Delany, Paul
       "Joyce's Political Development and the Aesthetic of
       Dubliners", *College English*, 34 (1972), 256–66

       Stresses the importance of the political and social aspects of
       lower middle-class Dublin life to *Dubliners*.

F57   Davis, William V.
       "The loss of time in 'Counterparts'", *James Joyce Quarterly*,
       10:3 (Spring 1973), 336–9

       Traces numerous references to time in this story as symbolizing
       an oppressive force.

F58   Stern, Frederick C.
       "'Parnell is Dead': 'Ivy Day in the Committee Room'",
       James Joyce Quarterly, 10:3 (Spring 1973), 228–39

       Interprets this story by keeping the historical figure of Parnell
       as the central focus and fitting peripheral details, such as the
       popping corks, to that focus.

F59   Walzl, Florence L.
       "Joyce's 'The Sisters': A Development", *James Joyce
       Quarterly*, 10:4 (Summer 1973), 375–421

       Looks at five versions of "The Sisters" in relation to Joyce's
       developing concept of *Dubliners*. The chief aims are: (1) to
       re-evaluate the original *Homestead* version; (2) to determine
       what changes were made in the story for it to serve as an
       introduction to *Dubliners*; and (3) to scrutinize the revisions as
       they bear upon meaning in "The Sisters", especially the typal
       or symbolic significance of the characters in the story.

F60   Somerville, Jane
       "Money in *Dubliners*", *Studies in Short Fiction*, 12 (1975),
       109–16

Examines the crucial significance of money not only as an indication of status and personal identity but as emblematic of social and sexual decadence.

F61   Leatherwood, A. M.
"Joyce's Mythic Method: Structure and Unity in 'An Encounter'", *Studies in Short Fiction*, 13 (1976), 71–8

Examines archetypal patterns of quest and of a child's transition to adulthood which give a mythic unity to "An Encounter".

F62   Walzl, Florence L.
"The Life Chronology of *Dubliners*", *James Joyce Quarterly*, 14:4 (Summer 1977), 408–15

Discusses Joyce's life chronology design (childhood, adolescence, maturity and public life) of the stories in the 1906 version of *Dubliners* and comments on its inconsistencies and complexities. Apparent contradictions in chronological groupings of stories are explained by Joyce's awareness and use of classical Roman divisions in the life span.

F63   West, Michael, and William Hendricks
"The Genesis and Significance of Joyce's Irony in 'A Painful Case'", *ELH*, 44 (1977), 701–27

Challenges a simplistic reading which assigns blame for Mrs Sinico's death to Mr Duffy. By drawing a parallel between "A Painful Case" and George Moore's novella "John Norton", the authors argue for a central irony in the story that makes the ending comic rather than tragic.

F64   Benstock, Bernard
"Joyce's Rheumatics: The Holy Ghost in *Dubliners*", *Southern Review*, 14 (1978), 1–15

Traces the subtle references throughout *Dubliners* to the Holy Ghost as Joyce's method for depicting the conspicuous lack of spirituality in turn-of-the-century Dublin.

F65   French, Marilyn
        "Missing Pieces in Joyce's *Dubliners*", *Twentieth Century
        Literature*, 24 (1978), 443–72

        An extended study of the *Dubliners* stories.

F66   Russell, John
        "James Joyce: *Dubliners*", STYLE IN MODERN BRITISH
        FICTION: STUDIES IN JOYCE, LAWRENCE, FOSTER,
        LEWIS, AND GREEN (Baltimore: Johns Hopkins
        University Press, 1978), pp. 17–42

        Although Russell reveals a rather limited notion of rhetoric,
        restricting his considerations to the "expressive experience", he
        finds several revealing stylistic patterns in the stories through
        his analysis of Joyce's use of the colon, semicolon (formal
        compounding), cadence, and the like.

F67   Cope, Jackson I.
        "Joyce's Waste Land", *Genre*, 12:4 (1979), 505–42

        A comparison of this essay with one by Staley (F69) provides
        an example of how divergent the criticism of *Dubliners*
        continues to be. Cope, in contrast to Staley, sees the work as
        an extension of nineteenth-century roots.

F68   Chesnutt, Margaret
        "Joyce's *Dubliners*: History, Ideology, and Social Reality",
        Eire, 14:2 (1979), 533–49

        A clear treatment of the historical, social and ideological
        context of the *Dubliners* stories.

F69   Staley, Thomas F.
        "A Beginning: Signification, Story and Discourse in Joyce's
        'The Sisters'", *Genre*, 12:4 (1979), 533–49

        A concentrated analysis of the first paragraph of "The Sisters",
        demonstrating theoretical possibilities in the methods of
        Todorov, Genet, and Barthes, along with glances at Maria
        Corti and Edward Said. See Cope (F67) for a different critical
        view.

F70   Voelker, Joseph C.
        "'He lumped the Emancipates Together': More Analogues for
        Joyce's Mr Duffy", *James Joyce Quarterly*, 18 (1980), 23–34

        This article acknowledges the presence in "A Painful Case" of
        parallel protagonists and situations which Joyce has faintly
        adumbrated in the text of the story.

F71   Morrisy, L. J.
        "Joyce's Narrative Strategies in 'Araby'", *Modern Fiction
        Studies*, 28:1 (Spring 1982), 45–52

        Challenges the structuralist notion that the identification of a
        narrator is not a valid critical ploy. Morrisey traces narrative
        shifts from third to first person in "Araby" as a way of
        explaining the different moods of the main character.

F72   Voelker, Joseph C.
        "'Chronicles of Disorder': Reading the Margins of Joyce's
        Dubliners", *Colby Library Quarterly*, 18:2 (June 1982),
        126–144

        Argues that rather than presenting the affliction of paralysed
        will, Joyce portrays his characters as incessant wanderers who,
        in the process of straying beyond the bounds of conventional
        respectability, are rewarded with insight.

F73   Smith, Paul
        "Crossing the Lines in 'A Painful Case'", *Southern
        Humanities Review*, 17:3 (Summer 1983), 203–8

        Avoids the common interpretation of Duffy as a misogynist
        along the lines of Nietzsche's Zarathustra. Instead, Smith
        turns to the more ambiguous Nietzschean position toward
        women in *A Gay Science*, suggesting that the Duffy/Sinico
        opposition in the story is a dialectic tension between the frailty
        of masculine "truth" and the power of feminine "illusion".

F74   Bremen, Brian A.
        "'He was Too Scrupulous Always': A Re-Examination of
        Joyce's 'The Sisters'", *James Joyce Quarterly*, 22:1 (Fall
        1984), 55–66

Summarizes previous scholarship in a succinct and deft way, at the same time highlighting certain points of Joyce's revisions of the story which more effectively brought out the relationship between the priest and the boy. This essay develops the argument that Father Flynn's sin is not so much one of simony as it is scrupulosity, a paralytic vice with which he has also infected the boy.

F75   Mandel, Jerome
       "The Structure of 'Araby'", *Modern Language Studies,* 15:4
       (Fall 1985), 48–54

Presents the argument that in "Araby" Joyce is working consciously within the literary convention of the medieval romance, and that the structure of the story corresponds to a paradigm of the Grail quest. The author draws comparisons with the chivalric tales of such medieval authors as Chrétien de Troyes, Gottfried von Strassburg and Wolfram von Eschenbach.

F76   Senn, Fritz
       "'The Boarding House' Seen as a Tale of Misdirection",
       James Joyce Quarterly, 23:4 (Summer 1986), 405–413

The narrative structure of this story is viewed as a series of several disjunct, incomplete versions of the relationship between Bob Doran and Polly Mooney. The effect of this narrative strategy is to misdirect continually the reader away from a clear grasp of the events of the story, thus subverting the clichés of romantic love.

F77   Norris, Margot
       "Narration Under a Blindfold: Reading Joyce's 'Clay'",
       PMLA, 102:2 (March 1987), 207–215

A reading of "Clay" which takes account of deceptive narrative gaps within which a reader constructs false images of Maria, viewing her as a witch, an asexual madonna or old maid. Such narrative superimpositions implicate the reader in the same societal prejudices which deprive Maria of any satisfactory role in life. This essay offers a perceptive and original perspective by a critic informed of current theoretical trends.

A Portrait of the Artist as a Young Man

Many of the works in the general studies section which take up the question of Joyce's aesthetic theories deal with *Portrait* in some detail and should be consulted.

See also: A9, B27, B41, D4, D6, D8, D10, D12, D15, D19, D24, D26, D28, D30, D31, D32, D45, D46, D64, D72, D73, D82, D98, D111, D113, D126, D135, D136, D160 and F1.

G1   Feehan, Joseph, ed.
DEDALUS ON CRETE: ESSAYS ON THE
IMPLICATIONS OF JOYCE'S *PORTRAIT* (Los Angeles:
St Thomas More Guild, Immaculate Heart College, 1957; rpt
1964)

A collection of original essays by various hands, aimed primarily at students. Although most of the material is dated, the essay by J. P. Nims remains lively. Perhaps the most distinguishing feature of this volume is the cover on which one of Sister M. Corita's first book cover designs appears.

G2   Connolly, Thomas E., ed.
JOYCE'S *PORTRAIT*: CRITICISM AND CRITIQUES
(New York: Appleton-Century-Crofts, 1962)

Brings together previously published essays on *A Portrait* and contains a special section dealing with Stephen's aesthetic theory. Includes pieces by H. M. McCluhan, Harry Levin, Hugh Kenner, Richard Ellmann and C. G. Anderson.

G3   Morris, William E., and Clifford A. Nault, eds
PORTRAITS OF AN ARTIST: A CASEBOOK ON
JAMES JOYCE'S *A PORTRAIT OF THE ARTIST AS A
YOUNG MAN* (New York: Odyssey, 1962)

Another collection which contains previously published essays. Besides interpretative essays dealing with the character of Stephen Dedalus, there is a section by Richard Ellmann on biographical aspects of *A Portrait*. Also included are numerous essays on Joyce's aesthetic theory and use of literary devices. Many of these essays are dated, though some, such as Hugh Kenner's "A Portrait in Perspective", are lasting statements on the novel.

G4   Ryf, Robert S.
A NEW APPROACH TO JOYCE: *THE PORTRAIT OF THE ARTIST* AS A GUIDE BOOK (Berkeley and Los Angeles: University of California Press, 1962)

Insists on the centrality of *A Portrait* in Joyce's art. Ryf sees the themes and techniques of the novel as embodying, in their expanded forms, all of Joyce's work. His theory that Joyce uses Stephen's aesthetic theories in his later work has been largely and correctly discounted. Ryf's observations on certain cinematic techniques employed in *A Portrait*, however, are revealing. His book is a reaction to certain critical assumptions that had minimized the *Portrait*, but his claims are far too strong and ignore the growing aesthetic subtleties and larger dimensions of the later work.

G5   Scholes, Robert, and Richard M. Kain, eds
THE WORKSHOP OF DAEDALUS: JAMES JOYCE AND THE RAW MATERIALS FOR *A PORTRAIT OF THE ARTIST AS A YOUNG MAN* (Evanston, Ill.: Northwestern University Press, 1965)

Noteworthy for making available study tools useful to both scholar and beginner. Manuscript materials are provided including transcriptions of Joyce's notebooks written before and during *A Portrait's* composition, an early and late draft of the novel, and a portion of Stanislaus Joyce's diary. There is a biographical section on Joyce's early years and selections from major writers who influenced Joyce. A valuable source book for the study of the shaping of Joyce's early work.

G6   Gifford, Don, and Robert J. Seidman
JOYCE ANNOTATED: NOTES FOR *DUBLINERS* AND *A PORTRAIT OF THE ARTIST AS A YOUNG MAN* (1967; 2nd edn, Berkeley, Los Angeles and London: University of California Press, 1982)

This substantially revised and expanded edition (which replaces the 1967 edition) is a very useful reference work for the study of *A Portrait*. Gifford not only annotates allusions and nuances of vocabulary, but provides maps which indicate the locales in *A Portrait*. The revised edition is also arranged to follow more closely the actual subdivisions in the *Portrait* chapters. As in the first edition, background information on the Dublin milieu is provided in the introduction.

G7   "Portrait Issue", *James Joyce Quarterly*, 4:4 (Summer, 1967), 249–356

A special issue, edited by Richard Kain, which presents various aspects of *Portrait* scholarship. Among the items included are a short note by Harry J. Pollock on Eileen Vance. Brian Dibble accounts for parallels between Joyce and Bruno; Thomas Zaniello reveals the many different applications for the term epiphany; and Eugene R. August examines Joyce's view of Irish Catholicism as shown through Stephen Dedalus and Father Arnall in the third chapter of *A Portrait*. As for structure in the book, Sidney Feshbach in his intriguing essay, notes the novel is organized around a traditional progression of character called "the ladder of perfection" and that Joyce has made Stephen's soul the soul and form of the novel. The character of Stephen is a topic of several essays. As for Joyce's relation to Stephen, Thomas W. Grayson suggests that the novel itself "serves to exorcise Stephen from the personality of Joyce, thereby permitting the emergence of the artist". James Naremore also interprets Dedalus and, more specifically, the technical problems posed by *A Portrait* with regard to irony and point of view. Parvin F. Sharpless summarizes the debate over ironic perspective in the character of Stephen instigated by the critics Hugh Kenner, Robert Scholes and Wayne Booth. Sharpless' view on the subject is that either the novel does not provide enough information to judge Stephen or that the information is so ambiguous as to allow any interpretation. Sharpless concludes that the remote artistic aspirations of Stephen make it difficult for critics to sympathize with his struggle, and this leads to harsher judgements, such as in the case of Kenner, than are called for.

G8   Anderson, Chester G., ed.
A *PORTRAIT OF THE ARTIST AS A YOUNG MAN*: TEXT, CRITICISM, AND NOTES (New York: Viking, 1968)

In addition to the text of the novel itself, this volume contains selections of criticism, detailed explanatory notes and selected bibliography. The criticism provides a valuable summary of the controversy over Joyce's relationship to and attitude toward Stephen Dedalus. Two essays by Wayne Booth and Robert Scholes present summary views and offer representative opposing conclusions. Booth concludes that the critical uncertainty surrounding Joyce's attitude toward Stephen's vocation, his aesthetics and his villanelle, reflects Joyce's own uncertainty; the text itself combines "irony and admiration in unpredictable mixtures". Scholes, conversely, offers ample evidence that the text can yield a predictable mixture. Using both external and internal evidence, he concentrates on an analysis of the villanelle, refutes Booth's position, and challenges the early position of Kenner (in *Dublin's Joyce*) which ascribes to Joyce an ironic vision.

G9   Epstein, Edmund L.
THE ORDEAL OF STEPHEN DEDALUS: THE
CONFLICT OF THE GENERATIONS IN JAMES
JOYCE'S *A PORTRAIT OF THE ARTIST AS A YOUNG
MAN* (Carbondale: Southern Illinois University Press, 1971)

The fullest treatment on subjects related to Stephen Dedalus. Especially valuable is the description of the way themes introduced in *A Portrait* are developed, refined and expanded in *Ulysses* and *Finnegans Wake*. Epstein's close and careful reading of the novel offers the best account thus far on the nature and source of Joyce's irony in the first section of Chapter 4 of *A Portrait*, but this delineation is not sustained for the latter portion of the novel. Epstein also offers an extended analysis of Stephen's lecture on aesthetics in Chapter 5 in light of the King David figure, the mature artist in the *Wake*. Epstein reads the book with an essentially optimistic ending—Stephen is confirmed in his vocation as artist and is reaching for maturity as a man. He is careful to point out, however, the clear limitation in Stephen's character at the conclusion of the novel, seeing Stephen as being too confident of his own powers and not aware of how confused some of his ideas are.

G10   Brown, Homer Obed
JAMES JOYCE'S EARLY FICTION: THE BIOGRAPHY
OF FORM (Cleveland, Ohio: Case Western Reserve
University, 1972)

Addresses in detail the problem of the success of *Dubliners* and Joyce's growing recognition of the artistic failure of *Stephen Hero*. Brown argues that changes in the formal development of the early work make possible the later evolutions in style; Joyce's changing concept of the nature of reality accounts for the shift from the early realism of the first stories of *Dubliners* and *Stephen Hero* to "The Dead" and *A Portrait*. "The Dead" signals a crucial stage of Joyce's development, Brown argues, for with it he was able for the first time to harmonize disparate visions of reality, fusing the cold and distant observer of a dead world and the symbolist poet who sought spiritual transcendence. "The Dead" looks forward to the world of *A Portrait* with its organic unity "held together by a narrator who represents both sides of this dualism". Many critics, in agreement with Brown, have explored this question from a biographical point of view, but Brown has given the question uniquely careful and logical analysis.

G11   Beja, Morris, ed.
JAMES JOYCE: *DUBLINERS* AND *A PORTRAIT OF THE ARTIST AS A YOUNG MAN: A CASEBOOK*
(London: Macmillan, 1973)

Contains not only critical responses to the text, but also background material such as manuscript excerpts and early reviews to *A Portrait*. The essays include Hugh Kenner's "The *Portrait* in Perspective", contributions by Harry Levin and Maurice Beebe on aesthetics in *A Portrait*, and a piece by Wayne Booth on Joyce's attitude toward Stephen. Most of these essays have been widely reprinted.

G12   Halper, Nathan
THE EARLY JAMES JOYCE (New York: Columbia
University Press, 1973)

An idiosyncratic introduction to Joyce that offers a concise analysis of his early accomplishments in the context of the later work and cautions the reader about various interpretive pitfalls. An engaging, interesting study.

G13   Sucksmith, Harvey P.
JAMES JOYCE: *A PORTRAIT OF THE ARTIST AS A*

YOUNG MAN (London: Arnold, 1973)

Designed as a starting point of critical exploration for the beginner.

G14   Staley, Thomas F., and Bernard Benstock, eds
APPROACHES TO JOYCE'S *PORTRAIT*: TEN ESSAYS
(Pittsburgh: University of Pittsburgh Press, 1976)

The book includes Staley's essay on *Portrait* scholarship, Hans Walter Gabler's history of the text, Breon Mitchell's essay on the relation of *Portrait* to the tradition of the *bildungsroman*, James Naremore's quasi-Marxist approach, Chester Anderson's uncompromising Freudian reading, Hugh Kenner's well-known and updated "The Cubist Portrait", Benstock's extensive essay on the symbolic structure, and Darcy O'Brien's "In Ireland after *A Portrait*". The volume provides a multiplicity of approaches to the novel, and many of the essays give prominence to the best previous scholarship on the various perspectives. All of the essays are original, written for this volume, except for Kenner's which was updated for the volume.

G15   Smith, John Bristow
IMAGERY AND THE MIND OF STEPHEN DEDALUS:
A COMPUTER-ASSISTED STUDY OF JOYCE'S *A PORTRAIT OF THE ARTIST AS A YOUNG MAN*
(Lewisburg, Pa: Bucknell University Press, 1980)

With the assistance of a computer, Smith traces developments in the character of Stephen according to changing patterns of imagery. The author claims the computer enables critics to grasp the comprehensive structure of imagery over an entire book rather than dwelling on localized clusters. It can be argued that a sensitive reader is already alert to a comprehensive image system, but the complexity of associations in *A Portrait* make Smith's study more than just a marginal contribution to Joyce studies.

G16   Bidwell, Bruce, and Linda Heffer
THE JOYCEAN WAY. A TOPOGRAPHIC GUIDE TO
DUBLINERS AND *A PORTRAIT OF THE ARTIST AS*

A YOUNG MAN (Baltimore: Johns Hopkins University Press, 1982)

(See F11 for annotation.)

G17   Buttigieg, Joseph A.
       A PORTRAIT OF THE ARTIST IN DIFFERENT
       PERSPECTIVE (Athens: Ohio University Press, 1987)

An important study that challenges much of the previous criticism of *A Portrait* by insisting on a different perspective. The author challenges certain assumptions regarding modernism and narrative that were a part of most previous Joyce scholarship. He attempts a critical reconsideration of Joyce's work and focuses on *Portrait* in order to re-evaluate the orthodox version of modernism. He locates in the work itself what he believes to be "a severe critique of the central tenets of new criticism—a critical approach that established itself in the mainstream of Joyce scholarship". The author's polemical tone, influenced by his reliance upon Nietzsche's view of history, is a deliberate part of his method. His discussions of Stephen Dedalus contain thorough analysis of the philosophical assumptions behind previous criticism that insists upon irony. The chapter on "The Religious Context" is an informed and thorough analysis of Joyce's use of Ignatius and Aquinas and an important reconsideration of these basic aspects of Joyce's novel. This study is a significant work that must be engaged by future critics of *Portrait*, if not Joyce's work generally.

Articles and Chapters in Books

G18   Kenner, Hugh
       "The *Portrait* in Perspective", JAMES JOYCE: TWO
       DECADES OF CRITICISM, ed. Seon Givens (1948; rev.
       edn, New York: Vanguard Press, 1963), pp. 132–74

This seminal essay, widely reprinted, is perhaps the single most influential study of the novel and became the starting place for most commentaries on *A Portrait* for twenty years. Kenner asserts that *A Portrait*, *Ulysses* and *Finnegans Wake* are all the same essential story told in differing modes and degrees of completeness. From this perspective, Kenner argues that correlations must be drawn between these three works for a complete rendering of Joyce's intent, that being to demonstrate a growing enlightenment of sensibility which ends with the comic spirit of *Finnegans Wake*. Much of Kenner's discussion in this essay focuses on the character of Stephen, whence derives the interpretation that Stephen cannot be conflated with Joyce and must be viewed, as did the author, with ironic detachment.

G19   Schorer, Mark
        "Technique as Discovery", *Hudson Review,* 1 (1948), 67–87

Describes the aesthetic achievement of *A Portrait* in terms of technique. Schorer argues that *A Portrait* "analyzes its material rigorously, and it defines the value and the quality of its experience not by appended comment or moral epithet, but by the texture of the style". Joyce's success, Schorer points out, was achieved by refining himself out of existence; that is, by refusing any overt commentary on the content of the novel. By the texture of the style Joyce defines the value and quality of experience in the novel. An early example of the "new criticism" approach applied to prose fiction.

G20   Anderson, Chester G.
        "The Sacrificial Butter", *Accent,* 12 (1952), 3–13.

Concentrates on two symbolic themes in Chapter 5: the poet as creator/God/father figure and the betrayal/crucifixion theme. Anderson stresses how Stephen's commonplace actions in this chapter can be interpreted as gestures associated with the celebration of Mass, with a Judas-like betrayal, and with the crucifixion. (Reprinted in G2 and G3.)

G21   Lind, Ilse Dusoir
        "*The Way of All Flesh* and *Portrait of the Artist as a Young Man*: A Comparison", *Victorian Newsletter,* 9 (1956), 7–10

Emphasizes that the shift from a Victorian text such as Samuel Butler's to a modernist text is a matter of change from the nineteenth-century intellectual occupations of *The Way of All Flesh* to the purely aesthetic focus of *A Portrait*.

G22   Beebe, Maurice
"Joyce and Aquinas: The Theory of Aesthetics", *Philological Quarterly*, 36 (January 1957), 20–35

Scrutinizes the extent to which Joyce follows Aquinas as an artistic programme, concluding that Joyce does incorporate the principles of Thomist philosophy but denies the supernatural beliefs on which they are based. The essay is especially useful for its detailed analysis of Stephen's version of Aquinas versus the original doctrine. (Reprinted in G2 and G11.)

G23   Redford, Grant H.
"The Role of Structure in Joyce's *Portrait*", *Modern Fiction Studies*, 4 (1958), 21–30

Redford suggests that the themes of search and rebellion in the book are made meaningful through structure, and "structure is the embodiment of an artistic proposition proclaimed by the central character himself as being basic to a work of art." (Reprinted in G2 and G3.)

G24   Boyd, Elizabeth F.
"Joyce's Hell Fire Sermons", *Modern Language Notes*, 75 (1960), 561–71

On the subject of the retreat sermon of Chapter 3. (Reprinted in G3.)

G25   Thrane, James R.
"Joyce's Sermon on Hell: Its Sources and Its Background", *Modern Philology*, 57 (1960), 172–98

Dealing with the retreat sermon of Chapter 3, this article shows conclusively that the sermons Father Arnall gives were borrowed by Joyce from Giovanni Pietro Pinomonti's *L'Inferno Aperto*, or *Hell Opened to Christians* in its nineteenth-century English translation. Compared with Boyd's (G24) treatment of the same subject, a superior piece. (Reprinted in D23.)

G26   Booth, Wayne C.
"The Problem of Distance in *A Portrait of the Artist*", THE

RHETORIC OF FICTION (Chicago: University of Chicago Press, 1961), pp. 324–36

Presents the observation that the critical uncertainty surrounding Joyce's attitude towards Stephen's vocation, his aesthetics and his villanelle reflects Joyce's own uncertainty. This section of Booth's book has been widely reprinted in anthologies of Joyce criticism, and its particular argument has been widely attacked. (Reprinted in G8 and G11.)

G27   Doherty, James
        "Joyce and *Hell Opened to Christians*: The Edition He Used for His Hell Sermons", *Modern Philology*, 61 (1963), pp. 110–19

        Compares the sermon of Father Arnall with the exact translation of Pinomonti's *Hell Opened to Christians* that Joyce used.

G28   Andreach, Robert J.
        "James Joyce", STUDIES IN STRUCTURE: THE STAGES OF THE SPIRITUAL LIFE OF FOUR MODERN AUTHORS (New York: Fordham University Press, 1964), pp. 40–71

        Andreach contends that the structure of *A Portrait* is built upon the stages of the five-fold Christian division of the spiritual life, "with a difference—the order of the stages is reversed and the individual stages are inverted." Even with Joyce's obvious delight in reversing religious symbols, Andreach's pattern seems too neat and forces him to conclude his judgement of Stephen on a far too simplistic basis.

G29   Atherton, James S.
        "Introduction" and "Notes", *A PORTRAIT OF THE ARTIST AS A YOUNG MAN*, JAMES JOYCE (London: Heinemann, 1964), pp. ix–xxii; 239–58

        Good introduction and helpful notes by a well-known Joyce scholar.

G30   Burke, Kenneth
        "Fact, Inference, and Proof in the Analysis of Literary

Symbolism", TERMS FOR ORDER, ed. Stanley Edgar
Hyman (Bloomington: Indiana University Press, 1964), pp.
145–72

Treats the individual words of *A Portrait* as the basic "facts",
and "the essay asks how to operate with these 'facts', how to
use them as a means of keeping one's inferences under control,
yet how to go beyond them, for purposes of inference, when
seeking to characterize the motives and 'salient traits' of the
work, in its nature as a total symbolic structure." Primarily
theoretical, Burke's essay uses *A Portrait* as a test case for
establishing a *modus operandi* for the analysis of literary
symbolism, but in so doing illuminates the symbolic network
of the novel.

G31   Hardy, John Edward
       "Joyce's *Portrait*: The Flight of the Serpent", MAN IN THE
       MODERN NOVEL (Seattle: University of Washington
       Press, 1964), pp. 67–81

Concentrates on the dark side of the Daedalus myth suggested
by the Minotaur and the hidden shame of both Minos and
Daedalus. Hardy sees the struggle in Stephen between his
Oedipal drives, his desire for artistry and his lust as parallel to
Joyce's own struggle to redeem himself from baser serpent-like
impulses through writing.

G32   Hayman, David
       "*A Portrait of the Artist as a Young Man* and *L'Éducation
       Sentimentale*: The Structural Affinities", *Orbis Litterarum*,
       19 (1964), 161–75

Attempts to locate Joyce's *Portrait* more specifically within
the tradition of Flaubert. Hayman sees the novel *L'Éducation
Sentimentale*, with its systematically paired sequences of
antithetical epiphanies and the way Flaubert used autobiographical content, as crucial to Joyce's formulation of *A Portrait*.

G33   Hayman, David
       "Daedalian Imagery in *A Portrait of the Artist as a Young
       Man*", HERIDITAS: SEVEN ESSAYS ON THE MODERN
       EXPERIENCE OF THE CLASSICAL, ed. Frederick Will
       (Austin: University of Texas Press, 1964), pp. 33–54

A thorough study of the mythic framework of the novel, suggests the way myth gives dimension and force to Stephen's character. This essay also offers an extended analysis of the way in which the Daedalus myth gives structure to the entire novel.

G34   Scholes, Robert
       "Joyce and the Epiphany: The Key to the Labyrinth?",
       Sewanee Review, 72 (Winter 1964), 65–77

       Attempts to clarify Joyce's own understanding of the term epiphany and seriously questions whether the term deserves the crucial importance attached to it by Joyce critics.

G35   Van Laan, Thomas F.
       "The Meditative Structure of Joyce's *Portrait*", *James Joyce Quarterly*, 1:3 (Spring 1964), 3–13

       On the question of Stephen's development as the central ordering device Joyce used for *Portrait*. Van Laan argues that an analogous correspondence exists between the novel and Ignatius Loyola's *Spiritual Exercises* and that Joyce employs Loyola's pattern of meditation and spiritual exercise. Van Laan further contends that using this pattern offered Joyce a system of introspective focus in a design that integrated miscellaneous units into a meaningful whole.

G36   Sprinchorn, Evert
       "Joyce: *A Portrait of the Artist as a Young Man*: A Portrait of the Artist as Achilles", APPROACHES TO THE TWENTIETH CENTURY NOVEL, ed. John Unterecker (New York: Crowell, 1965), pp. 9–50

       Sprinchorn attempts to account for what he sees as Joyce's loss of sympathy for Stephen in Chapter 5, but it is not convincing. His study offers an elaborate if somewhat pretentious explication of the chapter and further attempts to show its integration with the other four chapters and its consistency with the overall structure and symbolic pattern of the novel as a whole.

G37   Connolly, Thomas E.
       "Kinesis and Stasis: Structural Rhythm in Joyce's *Portrait of the Artist*", *University Review* (Dublin), 3 (1966), 21–30

A provocative argument against two critical commonplaces in *Portrait* studies: that Stephen's aesthetic theory has no relation to Joyce's own theory, and that Stephen's theory has no connection with the creative principles of the novel itself. Connolly sees *A Portrait* as structured around the replacement of kinetic appetites (both spiritual and physical) by the stasis of aesthetic contemplation.

G38   Lemon, Lee T.
"*A Portrait of the Artist as a Young Man*: Motif as Motivation and Structure", *Modern Fiction Studies*, 12 (1966–7), 441–52

Lemon bases his methodology on the work of the Russian formalists and thus argues that it is Joyce's adroit handling of the various motifs that reveals Stephen's development and subsequently unifies the novel.

G39   Rubin, Louis D.
"A Portrait of a Highly Visible Artist", THE TELLER IN THE TALE (Seattle: University of Washington Press, 1967), pp. 141–77

This essay shows the influence of Wayne Booth's *The Rhetoric of Fiction*, specifically the distinction Booth makes between implied author and the actual author. Rubin explores how Joyce has created his fictive persona in *A Portrait*, a narrative stance that fails in Chapter 5 because Joyce allows his own personality to interfere. The essay also offers an explanation of the controversy over the extent Joyce has written irony into Stephen.

G40   Beja, Morris
"James Joyce: The Bread of Everyday Life", EPIPHANY IN THE MODERN NOVEL (Seattle: University of Washington Press, 1971), pp. 71–111

Treats the conception and function of the epiphany in a number of modern writers, and his discussion of Joyce's use of the epiphany is a valuable analysis.

G41   Fortuna, Diane
"The Labyrinth as Controlling Image in Joyce's *A Portrait of*

the Artist as a Young Man", *Bulletin of the New York Public Library*, 76 (1972), 120–80

Traces with careful attention to archaeological detail and mythic artifact the Daedalus myth together with its ritualistic associations. The most extensive treatment of the details of Joyce's mythic framework in *A Portrait*.

G42   Jones, David E.
"The Essence of Beauty in James Joyce's Aesthetics", *James Joyce Quarterly*, 10:3 (Spring 1973), 291–311

Examines the dispute over Aquinas in Stephen's aesthetic theory. The article explores Aristotle's *De Anima* and *Metaphysics* as the basis for Stephen's theory, questioning Joyce's own interpretation of Aristotle and Aquinas.

G43   Buckley, Jerome H.
"Portrait of James Joyce as a Young Aesthete", SEASON OF YOUTH: THE *BILDUNGSROMAN* FROM DICKENS TO GOLDING (Cambridge, Mass.: Harvard University Press, 1974), pp. 225–47

Sees Joyce as summing up, even as he transforms, the traditions of the nineteenth-century *bildungsroman* in *A Portrait*. Although many critics disagree with him, Buckley concludes that the ending of the novel, "like that of many of another bildungsroman, presents problems of indecision and inconclusiveness".

G44   Rossman, Charles
"Stephen Dedalus and the Spiritual-Heroic Refrigerating Apparatus: Art and Life in Joyce's *Portrait*", FORMS OF MODERN BRITISH FICTION, ed. Alan W. Friedman (Austin: University of Texas Press, 1975), pp. 101–31

A fully developed discussion of the relation between Stephen's aesthetic theory and the manner in which the aesthetics express Stephen's character and experience. Rossman contends that just as Stephen's discourse on Shakespeare in *Ulysses* reveals more about Stephen that it does about *Hamlet*, so too does the aesthetic theory reveal more about Stephen's character than has previously been recognized.

G45   Benstock, Bernard
        "The Temptation of St. Stephen: A View of the Villanelle",
        James Joyce Quarterly 14:1 (Fall 1976), 31–8

        Observations on the erotic imagination of Stephen which
        culminates in the dream-induced villanelle. Benstock specul-
        ates on the mysterious figure of E. C., bird imagery and the
        stages of inspiration leading to the villanelle.

G46   Lanham, Jon
        "The Genre of *A Portrait of the Artist as a Young Man* and
        'the rhythm of its structure'", *Genre*, 10 (1977), 77–102

        This article argues that generic misconceptions of *A Portrait*
        have led to largely spurious interpretations. Lanham redefines
        the book as a confessional form blended with artistic impulse,
        a form which seeks to express essential truths rather than
        autobiographical fact yet still allows artistic experimentation
        and ironic modes.

G47   Beebe, Maurice
        "The *Portrait* as Portrait: Joyce and Impressionism", IRISH
        RENAISSANCE ANNUAL, I, ed. Zack Bowen (Newark:
        University of Delaware Press, 1980), pp. 13–31

        Beebe explores the thesis that Stephen's sensibility is related to
        that of an Impressionist painter, which explains some of the
        more obscure and diaphanous effects in style and conscious-
        ness that Joyce achieves.

G48   Ellmann, Maud
        "Disremembering Dedalus: *A Portrait of the Artist as a
        Young Man*", UNTYING THE TEXT: A POST-
        STRUCTURALIST READER, ed. Robert Young (Boston:
        Routledge and Kegan Paul, 1981)

        Explores the *Portrait* text as a process of constant
        deterioration. In this sense, self-mutilation, dissolution of ego,
        and the destructive interplay of text and sexuality highlight
        this neo-Freudian, post-Lacanian, deconstructive interpre-
        tation of a novel destroying itself.

G49   Riquelme, John Paul
        "Pretexts for Reading and for Writing: Title, Epigraph, and
        Journal in *A Portrait of the Artist as a Young Man*", *James
        Joyce Quarterly*, 18:3 (Spring 1981), 301–21

        Discusses idiosyncratic digressions in *A Portrait*, including
        intertextuality and the notation of dates and places, in order to
        determine how much of the novel is a revelation of the creative
        process rather than a novel in the traditional sense.

G50   Kuder, Stephen R.
        "James Joyce and Ignatius of Loyola: The Spiritual Exercises
        in *A Portrait of the Artist*", *Christianity and Literature*, 31:2
        (1982), 48–57

        Discusses Stephen Dedalus' spiritual evolution while at Father
        Arnall's retreat. Concludes by speculating why Stephen rejects
        the sprituality offered by Father Arnall.

G51   McGrath, F. C.
        "Laughing in His Sleeve: The Sources of Stephen's
        Aesthetics", *James Joyce Quarterly*, 23:3 (Spring 1986),
        259–275

        Renews the ongoing debate over the nature of Stephen's
        aesthetics in *A Portrait*. The author avoids the usual
        concentration on Aristotle and Aquinas or turn-of-the-century
        aestheticism, instead tracing the main source of Stephen's
        theory to the German romanticism of Kant and Hegel,
        especially the latter.

Exiles

Exiles has evoked widely varying critical response and has frequently been studied for its place in Joyce's artistic development rather than as an individual dramatic work judged on its own merits.
See also: D45, D88, D98, D107, D149 and D158.

H1   Fergusson, Francis
        "*Exiles* and Ibsen's Work", *Hound and Horn*, 5 (1932), 345–53

        An early essay by an important drama critic, Fergusson's study offers an analysis of the play's affinities with Ibsen's drama and praises it for its dramatic substance.

H2   Farrell, James T.
        "*Exiles* and Ibsen", JAMES JOYCE: TWO DECADES OF CRITICISM, ed. Seon Givens (1948; rev. edn New York: Vanguard Press, 1963), pp. 95–131

        Shows how Joyce attempted to capture the mood of Ibsen.

H3   Kenner, Hugh
        EXILES, DUBLIN'S JOYCE (Bloomington: Indiana University Press, 1955), pp. 69–94

        Sets down the major critical concerns *Exiles* scholarship has followed to date—the influence of Ibsen's naturalism, the establishment of its place in Joyce's canon both in theme and subject matter, the treatment of the themes of betrayal and exile which obsessed Joyce.

H4   Magalaner, Marvin, and Richard M. Kain
        EXILES, JOYCE: THE MAN, THE WORK, THE REPUTATION (New York: New York University Press, 1956), pp. 130–145

Notes Joyce's indebtedness to Ibsen as well as the superficial autobiographical elements and points out that the play has suppressed personal undertones and that the Ibsenesque style inhibits the symbolic associations that colour Joyce's conceptions.

H5   Aitken, D. J. F.
"Dramatic Archetypes in Joyce's *Exiles*", *Modern Fiction Studies*, 4 (1958), 42–52

Argues that two "archetypal dramas" are played out by the four main characters in *Exiles* and that the play has its general meanings on two different thematic levels. On one of these, each of the protagonists has an archetypal personality. On the other level, Richard is the archetype of the conscience-forging artist pitted against all the others who represent different aspects of unregenerate Ireland. These schemes, while not totally convincing, give Aitken opportunities for commentary on the symbols and motifs that Joyce employed to illuminate his characters and their relationships with each other.

H6   Tindall, William York
EXILES, A READER'S GUIDE TO JAMES JOYCE (New York: Noonday, 1959), pp. 104–122

Ponders the questions of theme, motive, and meaning concluding that in spite of Joyce's ability to handle increasingly complex material, he had not as yet achieved the aesthetic distance needed, especially in the drama.

H7   Adams, Robert M.
"Light on Joyce's *Exiles*? A New MS, a Curious Analogue, and Some Speculations", *Studies in Bibliography*, 17 (1964), 83–105

Adams' speculations stem from the discovery of manuscript pages containing dialogue that was never incorporated into the text.

H8   Clark, Earl John
"James Joyce's *Exiles*", *James Joyce Quarterly* 6:1 (Fall 1968) 69–78

Traces several autobiographical elements as they develop into human relationships within the play and circumscribe thematic development.

H9   Tysdahl, Bjorn J.
EXILES, JOYCE AND IBSEN: A STUDY IN LITERARY INFLUENCE (Oslo: Norwegian Universities Press, 1968; New York: Humanities Press, 1968), pp. 87–101

Points out how unsystematic and incomplete Joyce's understanding of Ibsen was.

H10   Benstock, Bernard
"*Exiles*: 'Paradox Lust' and 'Lost Paladays'", *ELH*, 36 (1969), 739–56

Argues that the great interest of the play is in what it reveals of Joyce's developing art.

H11   MacNicholas, John
"Joyce's *Exiles*: The Argument for Doubt", *James Joyce Quarterly*, 11:1 (Fall 1973), 33–40

Takes issue with those whom MacNicholas believes have done a disservice to the play by studying it primarily as a commentary on Joyce's fiction. He maintains that the play represents an elaborately crafted surface which is necessary to the complex themes developed in the work, and that although Joyce's refusal to disclose to the audience certain knowledge of Robert and Bertha's actions has made the play more static, this uncertainty is not simply a vagueness of mood but a dramatisation of Richard's own crippling doubt.

H12   MacNicholas, John
JAMES JOYCE'S *EXILES*: A TEXTUAL COMPANION (New York and London: Garland, 1979)

A thorough treatment of the literary and personal background of *Exiles*. The author discusses matters of textual genesis, composition and publishing history, and explores the relationship between unpublished fragments and the final version of the play. Also included are emendations to both the fair copy text and the Penguin edition.

H13   Bauerle, Ruth
        A WORD LIST TO JAMES JOYCE'S *EXILES* (New York
        and London: Garland, 1981)

        Provides a master list for both the vocabulary of *Exiles* and
        Joyce's notes for the play, based on the Penguin edition. An
        additional feature is a word list for fragments of the play,
        which sheds some light on Joyce's creative choice for the final
        version.

H14   MacNicholas, John
        "The Stage History of *Exiles*", *James Joyce Quarterly*, 19:1
        (Fall 1981), 9–26

        This essay surveys the critical reviews of *Exiles* for the past
        sixty years and speculates on the dramatic qualities of *Exiles*
        as a stage play, rather than a literary curiosity.

Ulysses

Ulysses has become, with *The Waste Land*, the central text of literary modernism. There are few book-length studies of the modern novel that do not include some discussion of *Ulysses*. The works listed in this section, however, deal for the most part exclusively with *Ulysses*.
See also: B4, B27, B29, D4, D6, D8, D10, D12, D15, D23, D26, D27, D28, D30, D31, D32, D35, D51, D56, D57, D61, D64, D66, D68, D69, D76, D77, D80, D81, D82, D85, D89, D95, D98, D102, D103, D104, D111, D113, D127, D149, D151 and D160.

Books

I1   Smith, Paul Jordan
A KEY TO THE *ULYSSES* OF JAMES JOYCE (Chicago: Covici, 1927; repr. San Francisco: City Lights, 1970)

The first book-length study of *Ulysses* to be published, a slight volume that provides a narrative sketch of the novel and stresses the influence of the *Odyssey* and its importance to an understanding of *Ulysses*.

I2   Gilbert, Stuart
JAMES JOYCE'S "*ULYSSES*": A STUDY (London: Faber and Faber, 1930; 2nd edn, New York: Knopf, 1952)

This book sets out to answer the charge that *Ulysses* is a formless work, but in so doing Gilbert imposes a rigid and limiting structure on the novel. Gilbert first concentrates on the various sources upon which Joyce drew (including the esoteric doctrine of metempsychosis) and follows with a chapter-by-chapter commentary emphasizing the Homeric parallels. He also traces the motifs and notes their complex expansion as they appear and reappear throughout the novel. Gilbert defends the elaborate stylistic variations as justified by Joyce's adaptation of form to content to create an organic unity. Gilbert's study, of course, suffers from the defensive context in which it was written and from the weak appeal to authority (Joyce himself). His arguments occasionally tend to be descriptive rather than analytical. The book did, however, exert a large influence on *Ulysses* studies—an influence that was frequently off target because of its unbalanced emphasis. It is important to note that copies of *Ulysses* were not generally available when this book was published, hence the long quotations from the text.

I3   Kain, Richard M.
FABULOUS VOYAGER: JAMES JOYCE'S *ULYSSES* (Chicago: University of Chicago Press, 1947; New York: Viking, 1959)

The most thorough and detailed reading of *Ulysses* of its day. The book emphasizes the naturalistic details of the novel, showing how intricately they were interwoven to provide a rich, resonant and poetic tone. Kain's appendices offer lists of over 530 references to Leopold Bloom, a list of over 150 characters, a directory of Dublin addresses and an index of verbal motifs. Beyond setting the novel brilliantly within its own world and in Dublin, Kain emphasizes the human nature of the characters and the themes of alienation and of modern man's search for community. Kain's study was extremely influential; besides its eloquent arguments for the novel's human portrayal and modern themes, it also reveals the order and purpose of Joyce's awesome use of naturalistic detail.

I4   Loehrich, Rolf
THE SECRET OF *ULYSSES*: AN ANALYSIS OF JAMES JOYCE'S *ULYSSES* (McHenry, Ill.: Compass Press, 1953)

An eccentric Freudian looks at *Ulysses* as the most spiritually enlightened book in Western literature, replacing Christianity with a scheme for revelation. This book represents the worst aspects of psychological criticism with the chaotic associative method leading to fantasy. Studies such as this one, however, were not infrequent during the fifties and sixties.

I5   Thompson, Lawrance R.
A COMIC PRINCIPLE IN STERNE–MEREDITH– JOYCE (Oslo: University of Oslo British Institute, 1954; Norwood, Pa: Norwood Editions, 1978)

A theoretical treatment of the comic in *Ulysses*, that is earlier and less extensive than Hayman (1970).

I6   Stanford, William B.
THE *ULYSSES* THEME: A STUDY IN THE
ADAPTABILITY OF A TRADITIONAL HERO (1954; 2nd
edn Oxford: Blackwell, 1963; New York: Barnes and Noble,
1964; 2nd edn rev., New York: Barnes and Noble, 1968)

An excellent study of the Odysseus figure throughout history,
from Homer to Kazantzakis. The chapter on Joyce's use of the
Homer theme is excellent, but the entire book is valuable for
the background to *Ulysses*.

I7   Schutte, William
JOYCE AND SHAKESPEARE: A STUDY IN THE
MEANING OF *ULYSSES* (New Haven: Yale University
Press, 1957)

An extended study of the nature and use of Shakespeare's life
and work in *Ulysses*. Besides examining carefully the complex
network of Shakespearean allusions and themes, Schutte also
delineates the way in which these references illuminate and
reinforce the meanings of the major themes, such as Stephen's
concept of art and its relationship to life. Schutte's extended
treatment of the "Scylla and Charybdis" episode is valuable
for its analysis of the Shakespearean material. Whether one
agrees with his interpretive conclusions or not, no one has so
exhaustively covered the full range of Shakespeare material as
Schutte.

I8   Goldberg, S. L.
THE CLASSICAL TEMPER: A STUDY OF JAMES
JOYCE'S *ULYSSES* (London: Chatto and Windus, 1961)

Goldberg's book is frequently brilliant; for example, his
discussion of Stephen's growing aesthetic from *A Portrait*
through its articulation in "Scylla and Charybdis" may well be
the best written on the subject. One argues outside rather than
inside Goldberg's book; he states clearly in his introduction
the limitations of his study—he will not emphasize the
mechanical intricacies, the symbolic elements, or the
"psychological subtleties" in order "to focus attention on the
meaning ... [Joyce] creatively revealed in his material, upon
themes realized dramatically". It is not Goldberg's Leavisite
turn toward "moral enactment" that is disturbing, but rather
the suggestion that an evaluation of a novel such as *Ulysses*

can be made without emphasizing those elements which give the work its complexity and significance; for they reflect, together with the dramatised material, that "constant state of mind" in which Joyce says the romantic and classical tempers must rise. Nevertheless, this is a valuable, informed and, at times, brilliant work. It is a work to which many critics have turned to take up Goldberg's arguments.

I9   Litz, A. Walton
        THE ART OF JAMES JOYCE: METHOD AND DESIGN
        IN *ULYSSES* AND *FINNEGANS WAKE* (London: Oxford
        University Press, 1961)

With the publication of the Gabler edition of *Ulysses*, a great deal of scholarly discussion and debate has centred on the manuscripts and evolving versions of the text. Litz's study was one of the first to give serious attention to the various stages of composition of *Ulysses* as well as *Finnegans Wake*. His study offers a detailed and systematic account of the genesis and growth of the two works through a careful account of the stages of composition from rough draft through proof sheets. Litz's work is especially valuable for its insights into the overall design and creative process in these works. Litz concludes that there is not "one controlling design", but rather an evolving process through the various stages of composition. Consistently, however, Joyce's compositional process is one of accretion.

I10   Parr, Mary
        JAMES JOYCE: THE POETRY OF CONSCIENCE: A
        STUDY OF *ULYSSES* (Milwaukee, Wis.: Inland Press,
        1961)

A weak book in which the author attempts to reveal Charlie Chaplin as the real-life model for Leopold Bloom and maintains that both blend into the archetype of the common man. Besides the extremely dubious reading, Parr's is a discursive, wandering work.

I11   Adams, Robert Martin
        SURFACE AND SYMBOL: THE CONSISTENCY OF
        JAMES JOYCE'S *ULYSSES* (New York: Oxford University
        Press, 1962)

Offers a necessarily selective but penetrating investigation into the raw materials that went into the making of *Ulysses*. Adams stresses Joyce's consistency in using factual materials, and, while acknowledging his essential accuracy, discovers that Joyce often intentionally confused or blurred certain factual details to create or emphasize patterns or relationships, or to break down relationships and leave a deliberately grainy texture. Adams has made a few factual errors of his own which have been pointed out by reviewers and later commentators (e.g., see Robert Boyle's "A Note on Reuben J. Dodd as 'a dirty Jew'", *James Joyce Quarterly*, 1965; also Hart in *James Joyce's "Ulysses"*, 1968). Though Adams has a rather ambiguous opinion of *Ulysses*, his book points to an important shift in the textual criticism; it marked the presence of more critical rigour and less elaborate suggestive and associative readings which characterized much of the criticism of the 1950s.

I12   Sultan, Stanley
THE ARGUMENT OF *ULYSSES* (Columbus: Ohio State University Press, 1964)

A thorough rendering of the narrative detail, cogently tracing the relationship between the narrative, the symbolic and the thematic. Sultan is especially illuminating when he brings into sharp focus the interplay between the dramatic events and the symbolic patterns. The book follows a chapter-by-chapter analysis, giving an excellent account of the full growth and import of the novel. On the other hand, Sultan's view of Stephen's ultimate destiny seems almost arbitrary, his too loosely drawn thesis on the source of Bloom's conflict is disappointing in its limitations, and his rigid moral bias leads to a far too narrow and restricted interpretation of the major characters. Sultan's study remains valuable, however, for its close examination of the text.

I13   Blamires, Harry
THE BLOOMSDAY BOOK: A GUIDE THROUGH JOYCE'S *ULYSSES* (London: Methuen, 1966)

Designed primarily for students, the book provides a line-by-line commentary. Although there are a substantial number of misreadings of fact and interpretation, it is a detailed guide.

I14   Hart, Clive
JAMES JOYCE'S *ULYSSES* (Sydney: Sydney University
Press, 1968)

Provides brief introductions to various aspects of Joyce's art.
His second chapter offers a clear reading of the narrative line,
comments on the developing themes and concludes by
pointing to the limited degree of reconciliation achieved
between Bloom and Molly and Stephen's limited recognition
of common humanity. Hart's final chapter, mentioned
elsewhere, provides an excellent view of the major
developments and positions in *Ulysses* scholarship through the
mid-1960s.

I15   Thornton, Weldon
ALLUSIONS IN *ULYSSES*: AN ANNOTATED LIST
(Chapel Hill: University of North Carolina Press, 1968)

An indispensable reference tool, listing the literary, historical,
philosophical and theological allusions in the book. Some
corrections and additions to this list have been published in
the *James Joyce Quarterly*. It is a valuable, well-documented
work for scholar and student alike.

I16   Kreutzer, Eberhard
SPRACHE UND SPIEL IM *ULYSSES* VON JAMES
JOYCE (Bonn: H. Bouvier, 1969)

Deals with Joyce's play on words in the widest possible sense,
emphasizing the multiple functions and the literary traditions
of word play. His careful study, together with its long (150-
page) index of word-play and puns, manages to convey a sense
of the intricate texture of *Ulysses*.

I17   Hayman, David
ULYSSES: THE MECHANICS OF MEANING
(Englewood Cliffs, N.J.: Prentice Hall, 1970; rev. and
expanded edition, Madison; University of Wisconsin Press,
1982)

Designed primarily to serve the general reader as a descriptive
introduction, it fulfils this purpose admirably. To call
Hayman's book an introduction is not to demean it, for even

the most advanced student of *Ulysses* can profit from reading it. Hayman's opening chapter is especially valuable for its succinct discussion of the literary traditions out of which Joyce's ideas and work grew. It is in this book that Hayman coined the term "arranger" to account for Joyce's narrative strategies and point of view. The later edition adds a chapter-by-chapter account of the action line and an interesting chapter on developments in *Ulysses* scholarship through the 1970s.

I18   Schneider, Ulrich
DIE FUNKTION DER ZITATE IM *ULYSSES* VON JAMES JOYCE (Bonn: H. Bouvier, 1970)

A detailed inquiry into the functions of quotation (document-ation, parody, composition). His treatment of the Moses configuration remains the most comprehensive thus far.

I19   Staley, Thomas F., and Bernard Benstock, eds
APPROACHES TO *ULYSSES*: TEN ESSAYS (Pittsburgh: University of Pittsburgh Press, 1970)

A collection of original essays by various hands, that represents the broad range of interest as well as the persistent questions the novel continues to evoke. David Hayman takes up the critical controversy on Molly's extra-marital activities and argues she is having her first affair. Darcy O'Brien, on the issue of Molly's love life, admits that the list of twenty-five lovers is obviously exaggerated but sees her as a frequent adulteress. As for questions of technique and method, Weldon Thornton's essay points out that Joyce's major device in achieving an effective blend of naturalism and symbolism was his mythical, allusive method. Thorton goes on to suggest, perhaps too easily, that the method itself is its own theme, revealing the solipsism and depletion of modern life. An essay by Fritz Senn examines and closely compares seven translations of *Ulysses* into European languages. His study is an excellent commentary on the general problems of translation as well as a fascinating excursion into the myriad problems that the translator encounters when tackling *Ulysses*.

I20   Ellmann, Richard
ULYSSES ON THE LIFFEY (London: Faber and Faber, 1972; New York: Oxford University Press, 1972)

Ellmann's study attempts to show the precise way in which Joyce has drawn elements from both the classical and medieval mind "into modern experience so that they have a present rather than an atavistic life". Ellmann perceives the structural form of *Ulysses* as moving in groups of three episodes—three being the determining element of structure—and each group embracing thesis, antithesis and synthesis. He also proposes "that in every group of three chapters the first refers to space, the second has time in the ascendant, and the third blends (or expunges) the two". Ellmann has created a new schema out of the Gorman–Gilbert and Linati schemata, one he believes reflects more completely the aesthetic and moral dimensions of the novel. The author acknowledges little of the criticism since Gilbert. This omission gives the book a certain freedom and freshness, which is, of course, Ellmann's avowed purpose, but many of his insights have been suggested by earlier scholars.

I21   Field, Saul, and Morton P. Levitt
BLOOMSDAY: AN INTERPRETATION OF JAMES JOYCE'S *ULYSSES* (Greenwich, Conn.: New York Graphic Society, 1972)

Offers the engravings of Saul Field and a series of interpretive vignettes by Morton P. Levitt. Field's colour engravings, created by a unique process, attempt to capture visually the themes and characters of *Ulysses*, with signal emphasis given to Leopold Bloom. Levitt's essay is a competent contribution to the book, but it lacks focus. He seems unsure whether he is writing merely an accompanying text for Field's art, an introductory essay or one with more specialized focus.

I22   Herring, Phillip
JOYCE'S *ULYSSES* NOTESHEETS IN THE BRITISH MUSEUM (Charlottesville: University Press of Virginia, 1972)

Makes available the notesheets for the last seven episodes of *Ulysses* which reside in the British Museum. In addition to the transcribed notesheets, Herring provides a descriptive essay for each relevant chapter as well as footnotes to explain textual and interpretive issues raised by the notesheets. Manuscript study has become increasingly important in Joyce studies, not only as a tool for viewing Joyce's creative process, but for clarifying his intentions in a given passage.

I23   Mason, Michael
        JAMES JOYCE: *ULYSSES* (London: Arnold, 1972)

Brief introduction, very slight in comparison to the Hart and Hayman volumes.

I24   "*Ulysses* and *The Waste Land* Fifty Years After: A Critical Retrospective", *Mosaic* 6:1 (1972), 3–245

The essays on *Ulysses* are fairly general: Kain and Staley discuss the present stature of *Ulysses* and the evolution of the critical opinion respectively, Marvin Magalaner attempts to balance the negative interpretation of Stephen that has been rendered by many critics, and Chester Anderson argues that Joyce had close knowledge of Freud's *The Psychopathology of Everyday Life* and demonstrates this knowledge through the internal evidence found in the "Lestrygonian" episode. Anderson's essay is carefully documented and thoroughly investigated, and is the most significant of the *Ulysses* essays in the volume. Besides the obvious mutual publication year, it is appropriate that the *Mosaic* volume includes essays on *The Waste Land*, because the two works have been frequently compared over the years.

I25   Fischer-Seidel, Therese, ed.
        BEWUSSTSEINSDARSTELLUNG IM WERK VON
        JAMES JOYCE VON DUBLINERS ZU *ULYSSES*
        (Frankfurt am Main: Athenaeum Verlag, 1973)

A perceptive examination of how consciousness is actually presented and of the complex narrative devices employed in Joyce's work through *Ulysses*. Its tendency toward scientifically precise abstraction makes it difficult to read even for its German audience, but its precise terminology and its conceptual exactness represent an advance in Joyce scholarship, for no study in English, including Steinberg's (I26), offers such a sophisticated and thorough methodology in the analysis of Joyce's presentation of consciousness.

I26 Steinberg, Erwin R.
THE STREAM OF CONSCIOUSNESS AND BEYOND
IN *ULYSSES* (Pittsburgh: University of Pittsburgh Press,
1973)

The first full-scale treatment of this important aspect.
Drawing heavily upon psychology and on developments in the
other arts, he traces the historical development of the
technique in literature and analyses in systematic detail Joyce's
particular use of it. After describing generally Joyce's version,
Steinberg compares the streams-of-consciousness of Molly,
Bloom and Stephen, analysing sentence structure, word usage
and intellectual content. His study is based on the earlier
drafts as well as the final ones and reveals the careful and
elaborate way in which Joyce developed his character through
technique. His careful analysis of so many technical aspects of
the novel challenges the speculative, easy interpretations that
many critics have fallen prey to. Perhaps more importantly,
his study brings to light an area in Joyce's development that
heretofore had not been adequately taken into account. But
this study also raises questions concerning methodology of
analysis and the need for clearer premises.

I27 Bonnerot, Louis, ed.
ULYSSES: CINQUANTE ANS APRÈS (Paris: M. Didier,
1974)

Twenty-five essays covering a wide range of subjects on or
closely related to *Ulysses* by well-known critics from America
and Europe. Also included are the Gilbert, Gorman and Linati
schemata. Several of the essays are in French, but most are in
English.

I28 Bowen, Zack
MUSICAL ALLUSIONS IN THE WORKS OF JAMES
JOYCE: EARLY POETRY THROUGH *ULYSSES*
(Albany: State University of New York Press, 1974)

The major portion of this study is devoted to *Ulysses* with a
two-fold purpose: to provide a thorough annotation of
musical allusions in that work and to offer a unified critical
commentary on how Joyce used music to reinforce his
conceptions of style, character, structure and theme. Although
Joyce does not initiate any major themes with music, his

substantial use of popular and folk music, opera, music-hall songs and church music attests to the value Joyce placed on musical expression, not only as a system of cultural allusion, but as a stylistic device. In addition to over 700 allusions in *Ulysses*, Bowen's study also covers the sporadic use of music in Joyce's earlier works.

I29   Gifford, Don, with Robert J. Seidman
NOTES FOR JOYCE: AN ANNOTATION OF JAMES JOYCE'S *ULYSSES* (New York: Dutton, 1974)

This compilation includes allusions, Dublin addresses, translations of foreign words, definitions of slang terms, and maps of Dublin and Gibraltar. Although the book has many shortcomings, it is useful for the beginning student. The documentation is frequently too sketchy to be helpful to the specialist, and some material of marginal value is included. Also, most of the material from Thornton's *Allusions in Ulysses* is repeated, but the authors overlook a number of the subsequent discoveries and corrections that have appeared as brief notes in journals.

I30   Hart, Clive and David Hayman, eds
JAMES JOYCE'S *ULYSSES*: CRITICAL ESSAYS
(Berkeley and Los Angeles: University of California Press, 1974)

A most significant critical book on *Ulysses* that provides a solid narrative of the highlights of the major critical issues which evolved through the mid-sixties. Each of the eighteen contributors discusses one of the episodes; some of these essays have been referred to elsewhere in this volume. The contributors include Bernard Benstock on "Telemachus", Phillip F. Herring on "Lotus Eaters", Fritz Senn on "Nausicaa", Hugh Kenner on "Circe", and Robert Boyle on "Penelope". Although the essays are somewhat uneven in quality, most are rich with new ideas and information and show that new approaches can still be taken to the novel. One of the best and most important is Clive Hart's essay on "Wandering Rocks", which includes a discussion of the interpolations in the episode and a chart of the times and places mentioned, demonstrating Joyce's realistic precision. Another essay of note is Adaline Glasheen's essay on "Calypso", which balances with a great deal of wit Bloom's ten years of roaming against Molly's recent relationship and discusses his marital failures and his quest for other women.

I31 Shechner, Mark
JOYCE IN NIGHTTOWN: A PSYCHOANALYTIC
INQUIRY INTO *ULYSSES* (Berkeley and Los Angeles:
University of California Press, 1974)

This Freudian analysis is the most thoroughly psychoanalytic study of Joyce to date, concentrating on the web of family relationships in *Ulysses*, especially as they relate to Joyce's own personal life. Included are discussions on Stephen's Oedipal situation, Joyce's love letters to Nora, and the connection between Joyce's sexuality and Bloom's. The author also explores various women characters in *Ulysses*, with emphasis on Molly, and concludes with a final chapter on Joyce and his mother.

I32 Staley, Thomas F., ed.
ULYSSES: FIFTY YEARS (Bloomington: Indiana
University Press, 1974)

A collection of essays that originally appeared as the *James Joyce Quarterly Ulysses* anniversary issue (10:1, Fall 1972). Each author concentrates on a particular critical problem in *Ulysses* and attempts to view it from the perspective of fifty years. A. Walton Litz carefully argues that Pound's and Eliot's initial arguments have become large critical touchstones, and that *Ulysses* criticism can be seen as a continuing dialogue between the spiritual descendants of Pound and Eliot. William M. Schutte notes that scholarship on the early Bloom episodes is insubstantial but also summarizes the large majority of critical opinion when he concludes that the remarkably humane element of Bloom's character dominates the book. Hugh Kenner in "Molly's Masterstroke" asserts that Boylan is Molly's first lover, also suggesting her ambivalence over the act as she tries to avoid sexual intercourse with Boylan while inviting it. It is significant that a number of these essays in this volume stress close textual reading rather than broad interpretive or thematic studies, with the exception of Maurice Beebe's "*Ulysses* and the Age of Modernism", which offers a view of the novel in the broad context of modernism and argues for its centrality within the movement.

I33   Driver, Clive, ed.
        ULYSSES: A FACSIMILE OF THE MANUSCRIPT, 3
        vols (New York: Octagon, 1975)

        This is a facsimile reproduction of the 810-page holograph
        manuscript that is now owned by the Rosenbach Foundation.

I34   Hart, Clive, and A. M. Leo Knuth
         A TOPOGRAPHICAL GUIDE TO JAMES JOYCE'S
        ULYSSES, 2 vols (Colchester, England: *Wake Newslitter*
        Press, 1975)

        Includes an address list of the Dublin places mentioned in
        Ulysses, a discussion of Joyce's use of *Thom's Directory*, and
        eighteen detailed maps for the various episodes. It is an
        extremely useful work for the serious student of *Ulysses*.

I35   French, Marilyn
        THE BOOK AS WORLD: JAMES JOYCE'S *ULYSSES*
        (Cambridge, Mass.: Harvard University Press, 1976)

        This book takes issue with critics who have explored the
        structure of *Ulysses* in terms of themes, Homeric correspond-
        ence and character development. Dismissing the concept of a
        conventional plot, French develops the argument that
        structure in *Ulysses* is a matter of surface style and a
        fluctuating narrator who offers a succession of differing points
        of view. By offering a close chapter-by-chapter reading of the
        text, the author relates each narrational point of view to a
        structure that takes shape as a loose collection of momentary
        experiences existing not within the text itself but within the
        mind of a reader. French defines this structure in terms of
        concentric circles, analogous to Dante's *Divine Comedy*, in
        which the reader revolves in greater and greater vistas of
        allegorical perception, beginning in the particulars of Dublin
        city and expanding to the universal. *The Book as World* is
        based partly on reader response models of criticism, partly on
        close reading combined with the author's compassionate
        response to the human condition presented in *Ulysses*.

I36   Seidel, Michael
        EPIC GEOGRAPHY: JAMES JOYCE'S *ULYSSES*
        (Princeton: Princeton University Press, 1976)

Argues cunningly that Joyce repeats the epic geography of the *Odyssey* in *Ulysses* and does so according to the Homeric action as cartographed by Victor Bérard in *Les Phéniciens et L'Odyssée* (1902–3). Bérard's influence has long been acknowledged, but it has never been so comprehensibly accounted for, nor have its implications been so thoroughly discussed. Some of the elaborate charting and epic movement and placement seem inflated, even remote to the action, but Seidel's study is especially interesting for its discussion of mythology, philosophy and epic poetry generally, in the light of Bérardian parallels. *Epic Geography* is an intriguing source study.

I37   Fischer-Seidel, Therese, ed.
JAMES JOYCES *ULYSSES*: NEUERE DEUTSCHE AUFSÄTZE (Frankfurt am Main: Suhrkamp, 1977)

Collection of essays that contains contributions by Fritz Senn, Hans Gabler, Arno Esch, Franz K. Stanzel and Viktor Link, as well as an excellent bibliography of *Ulysses* studies.

I38   Raleigh, John Henry
THE CHRONICLE OF LEOPOLD AND MOLLY BLOOM: *ULYSSES* AS NARRATIVE (Berkeley and Los Angeles: University of California Press, 1977)

Intricate chronology of the lives of Leopold and Molly, which also includes lists of Bloom's addresses and jobs and more that half-dozen maps and diagrams of such things as the floor plan of 7 Eccles Street. Raleigh subtitles his work *"Ulysses" as Narrative*, because its year-by-year chronicle highlights, "as no other method could, the immense and detailed naturalistic base upon which *Ulysses* is constructed". Raleigh's task was not easy, because the naturalistic base itself has many conflicting facts, as one finds in the life it reflects. Leopold and Molly often disagree on what he or she did when. Raleigh, rather than speculate on who is right in the absence of further evidence, presents the conflicting facts. There are even more difficult problems in *Ulysses* that Raleigh must encounter, not the least of which is what consitutes evidence. Raleigh's chronology does not make a distinction between fictional and historical reality, but it is virtually complete. Raleigh puts the facts of the Blooms' life in order and, in so doing, gives the reader yet another, if partial, view of the controlled universe Joyce created in *Ulysses*.

I39   Sultan, Stanley
       ULYSSES, THE WASTE LAND, AND MODERNISM: A
       JUBILEE STUDY (Port Washington, N.Y.: Kennikat, 1977)

Does not dwell on what has now become a critical commonplace, the influence of *Ulysses* on *The Waste Land,* but looks at the two works together and sees them as the richest expression of modernism.

I40   Henke, Suzette
       JOYCE'S MORACULOUS SINDBOOK: A STUDY OF
       ULYSSES (Columbus: Ohio State University Press, 1978)

Proposes to examine *Ulysses* from a phenomenological and existential orientation. The results, however, are slightly disappointing. The work is not an informed example of phenomenology and its method, and Henke's prose is pretentious.

I41   Lobsien, Eckard
       DER ALLTAG DES *ULYSSES*: DIE VERMITTLUNG
       VON ÄSTHETISCHER UND LEBENSWELTLICHER
       ERFAHRUNG (Stuttgart: J. B. Metzler, 1978)

A sound phenomenologically oriented study that perhaps argues too strenuously with positivistic-oriented criticism.

I42   Maddox, James H.
       JOYCE'S *ULYSSES* AND THE ASSAULT UPON
       CHARACTER (London: Harvester Press, 1978; New
       Brunswick, N.J.: Rutgers University Press, 1978)

Emerges out of the critical environment of S. L. Goldberg's *The Classical Temper* (1961), with its emphasis on character and moral enactment. Maddox, whose study of character develops Goldberg's treatment of Joyce's aesthetic theories, proposes that Joyce's characterization is predicated on the coexistence of opposites, and furthermore, that his stylistic variations are the corollary of Stephen's axiom: "Proteus thought the world can be known only through refracted signatures." Goldberg can see no redeeming features in the stylistic narrative and extravagance of the last part of *Ulysses*, but Maddox can, through the "refracted signatures" and Joyce's profound faith in the individual. Proceeding from these propositions, Maddox's *Ulysses* becomes an integrated work, though not a schematized one. Maddox is a careful reader, and his book reflects a struggle for openness and precision.

I43 Sandulescu, Constantin-George
THE JOYCEAN MONOLOGUE: A STUDY OF CHARACTER AND MONOLOGUE IN JOYCE'S *ULYSSES* AGAINST THE BACKGROUND OF LITERARY TRADITION (Colchester, England: *Wake Newslitter* Press, 1979)

This study is needlessly rigid and at the same time discursive; it attempts to set Joyce's monologues and character development against the modern literary tradition. Sandulescu's treatment of Dorothy Richardson, for example, is inadequate for the conclusions he draws and his contentions regarding Joyce's influence on Svevo do not seem valid.

I44 Barrow, Craig Wallace
MONTAGE IN JAMES JOYCE'S *ULYSSES* (Madrid and Potomac, Md: Studia Humanitatis, 1980)

A study of how the film technique of montage is useful as a metaphor for examining both the objective and subject events of *Ulysses*. The author not only explores Joyce's style as a literary equivalent of montage, but also describes certain devices such as verb tense, that are unavailable in cinema.

I45 Caspel, Paul P. J. van
BLOOMERS ON THE LIFFEY: EISEGETICAL READINGS OF JAMES JOYCE'S *ULYSSES*, PART II (Groningen, Netherlands: Veenstra Visser, 1980; revised and enlarged edition, Baltimore: Johns Hopkins University Press, 1986)

This curious and enjoyable study examines a number of introductions and guidebooks to *Ulysses* for accuracy of information and finds an incredible number of misquotations and factual errors in all of them. Translations are in an equally bad state, as this interesting study reveals. The error-filled Random House text of *Ulysses* seems reliable by comparison.

I46   Gose, Elliott B., Jr
        THE TRANSFORMATION PROCESS IN JOYCE'S
        ULYSSES (Toronto: University of Toronto Press, 1980)

Emphasizes the influence of Bruno, Freud and Bergson on
Joyce and contends that their ideas helped Joyce develop his
own ideas about life as a process of transformation. While this
thesis may not be convincing and the study itself is uneven,
much of the discussion in this work is intelligent and
provocative.

I47   Gottfried, Roy K.
        THE ART OF JOYCE'S SYNTAX IN *ULYSSES* (Athens:
        University of Georgia Press, 1980)

A thorough and informative study of the diverse sentence
patterns in *Ulysses* and the stylistic variations that Joyce's
syntactical arrangements create. Gottfried's work is especially
valuable for the close attention it gives to Joyce's use of
various sentence patterns to form the different styles from
episode to episode and the way in which these styles reflect the
tension in the novel between freedom and order.

I48   Kenner, Hugh
        ULYSSES (London: Allen & Unwin, 1980; revised edition,
        Baltimore and London: Johns Hopkins University Press,
        1987)

This study brings the broad range of Kenner's ideas from
Dublin's Joyce, The Counterfeiters, The Pound Era, and
Joyce's Voices into perspective. Ever since his discussion of
"double writing" in *Dublin's Joyce,* Kenner has been
concerned with Joyce's rhetoric—its repetitions, its locutions,
its interwoven system of referents. Narrative idiom that need
not be the narrator's ("The Uncle Charles Principle") is also
prominent in this study. Kenner engages many questions of
style. Kenner re-examines the Homeric parallel and its
function—primarily ironic in the earlier chapters and
"coercive" in the last eight. Kenner's is not a complete and
systematic study that covers each episode; rather it is another
look at those aspects of *Ulysses* that continue to engage him
and that he judges the central concerns of the text. This is a
work by a major critic that modifies, reasserts, refocuses and
renews his reading and interpretation of a text, and the results

are important and enduring. References to *Ulysses* in the new edition are keyed to the Gabler edition.

I49   Almeida, Hermione de
BYRON AND JOYCE THROUGH HOMER: DON JUAN AND ULYSSES (New York: Columbia University Press, 1981)

Concentrates on the similarity between Joyce's *Ulysses* and Byron's *Don Juan* through the Homeric parallel. Both writers are analysed in terms of their transformation of epic elements into their respective ages, addressing the nature of heroism, functioning as social critics and relying on parody as a prime literary device.

I50   Delaney, Frank
JAMES JOYCE'S ODYSSEY: A GUIDE TO THE DUBLIN OF *ULYSSES* (London: Hodder and Stoughton, 1981; New York: Holt, Rinehart and Winston, 1981)

An impressionistic tribute to *Ulysses* following the sequence of its chapters. The author combines biographical, photographic and textual fragments as well as plot summary, to create a readable pictorial commentary. Photos include recent items by Jorge Lewinski and vintage selections from the Lawrence collection.

I51   Lawrence, Karen
THE ODYSSEY OF STYLE IN *ULYSSES* (Princeton: Princeton University Press, 1981)

Offers a reader-oriented analysis of *Ulysses* based on style instead of the more traditional approaches of myth, allusion, plot and character. The premise of the work is that *Ulysses* establishes a normative style of narration in the first six chapters, which is then disrupted by a radically different kind of writing. Lawrence defines this new style as a public exhibition, a narrative characterized by a memory which seizes upon, transforms and restates its prior utterance. Lawrence's analysis is sometimes stretched to accommodate literary theory rather than the text itself. But this study reflects the increased attention being given narrative aspects in Joyce.

152   Schutte, William M.
        INDEX OF RECURRENT ELEMENTS IN JAMES
        JOYCE'S *ULYSSES* (Carbondale: Southern Illinois
        University Press, 1982)

        This study investigates repeating words, phrases and ideas in
        the 1961 Random House edition of *Ulysses* by using a system
        that cross-references all words except proper names that
        appear frequently such as Bloom, Stephen, Molly. The work
        may help provoke recognition of recurrent elements in
        Ulysses, but the increasing importance of the Gabler edition
        makes Schutte's use of the Random House unfortunate.

153   Thomas, Brook
        JAMES JOYCE'S *ULYSSES*: A BOOK OF MANY
        HAPPY RETURNS (Baton Rouge: Louisiana State
        University Press, 1982)

        Self-consciousness and self-reflexivity in Joyce's work is
        investigated with a parallel discussion of critical approaches to
        literary theory, expecially reader-response. By focusing upon
        the reader's role in producing *Ulysses*, Thomas presents a
        substantial unveiling of textual mechanisms (such as style) in
        the novel. Language is the medium of this semiotic exchange
        in which Thomas attempts successfully to circumscribe "the
        book's tale of the telling rather than the book's naturalistic
        tale". Thomas asserts that this privileging of language enables
        the reader to see more easily the textual consciousness
        expressed by the novel, and that "trying to uncover *Ulysses'*
        meaning independent of its language is to indulge in the myth
        that our relation to the world is not conditioned by language."
        An interesting example of what reader-response criticism can
        contribute to Joyce studies. A work that comes out of
        Wolfgang Iser's theoretical studies.

154   Janusko, Robert
        THE SOURCES AND STRUCTURES OF JAMES
        JOYCE'S "OXEN" (Ann Arbor, Michigan: UMI Research
        Press, 1983)

        An intensive study of the narrative and thematic aspects of a
        difficult, multi-faceted chapter. Using manuscript evidence,
        the author traces the overall embryological framework and
        foetal characteristics which Joyce carefully worked in to

correspond to Mina Purefoy's labour. The book also addresses the crucial aspect of Joyce's stylistic parodies of English literature and the sources which influenced the composition of the chapter.

I55   Madtes, Richard E.
THE "ITHACA" CHAPTER OF JOYCE'S *ULYSSES* (Ann Arbor, Michigan: UMI Research Press, 1983)

Traces the growth of the "Ithaca" chapter of *Ulysses* through examination of the artifacts (manuscripts, notes, proofs, etc.) remaining from the composition process. Madtes argues that "for full understanding and appreciation" of both the novel as a whole and each individual chapter, "study of the text of one [chapter] 'as is' is not enough; one must also examine the text in the process of becoming."

I56   Card, James Van Dyck
AN ANATOMY OF "PENELOPE" (Rutherford, N. J.: Fairleigh Dickinson University Press, 1984; London and Toronto: Associated University Presses, 1984)

Analyses the development of the "Penelope" section of *Ulysses* through existing manuscript versions to demonstrate the fragmentary process Joyce followed and, more importantly, to highlight the underlying structural logic ("the mesh of the text") of Molly's monologue.

I57   Harkness, Marguerite
THE AESTHETICS OF DEDALUS AND BLOOM (Lewisburg: Bucknell University Press; London and Toronto: Associated University Presses, 1984)

An investigation of Joyce's aesthetics through the characters of Dedalus, Leopold, and to some extent, Molly Bloom. The author recapitulates much of what has already been covered on this subject as early as Edmund Wilson's *Axel's Castle*, but presents the intriguing yet scantily developed theory that Molly Bloom is the figure whose nature most represents Joyce's aesthetic habits.

I58   Tucker, Lindsey
STEPHEN AND BLOOM AT LIFE'S FEAST:

ALIMENTARY SYMBOLISM AND THE CREATIVE
PROCESS IN JAMES JOYCE'S *ULYSSES* (Columbus:
Ohio State University Press, 1984)

Examines the use of bodily functions as metaphors for the
creative process in *Ulysses*, primarily as they relate to Stephen
and Bloom. The emphasis upon the body allows for a fresh
approach to the fleshy reverberations of the novel as
demonstrated by, among other things, Joyce's assignment of
body parts for each chapter of what he called his "epic of the
human body". "Joyce uses both ritual and alchemy as sources
for imagery when he speaks of the creative process," Tucker
asserts, "and both ritual and alchemy are grounded in
alimentary functions." By focusing upon alimentary concerns
as they affect ingestion and transformation of materials into
energy, art and ritual, Tucker brings forth aspects of *Ulysses*
which previous critics have not explored extensively.

159   Kim, Chong-Keon
JAMES JOYCE: *ULYSSES* AND LITERARY
MODERNISM (Seoul, Korea: Tamgu Dang, 1985)

Examines *Ulysses* as a paradigm of literary modernism by
placing it within the artistic milieu of the period and
"exploring the nexus of [Joyce's] artistic theories and the
practice of them in the work". "As a crucial testing ground for
new theories and techniques of modern fiction," Kim observes,
"[Joyce's] novel is considered a demonstration and *summa* of
the major features of the entire movement." This study is
derivative but it reflects the sustained interest in Joyce by
Korean scholars. Kim is also the translator of *Ulysses* into
Korean.

160   Steppe, Wolfhard, with Hans Walter Gabler
A HANDLIST TO JAMES JOYCE'S *ULYSSES* (New York
and London: Garland Publishing, 1985)

Provides a complete alphabetical index to the Gabler edition
of *Ulysses* (published in 1984). The *Handlist* is designed to
meet the need for orientation in locating individual words,
symbols and numbers in the new text. It is not intended as a
dictionary or critical commentary on the vocabulary of
Ulysses, nor as a guide to the synoptic text, but as a reliable
indicator of the location of "graphic units" in the critically
established reader text.

Sandulescu, C.-H. George, and Clive Hart, eds
ASSESSING THE 1984 *ULYSSES* (Gerrards Cross, Bucks:
Colin Smythe, 1986; Totowa, N.J.: Barnes and Noble, 1986)

A collection of essays which addresses various textual issues
surrounding the Gabler computer-generated *Ulysses*. The
essays offer a largely negative response to the Gabler edition.
Among the issues discussed is Richard Ellmann's unfavour-
able response to the restoration of the passage from "Scylla
and Charybdis" which mentions the word "love". Also
addressed is the problem of Gabler's construction of an ideal
copy text out of pre-publication materials. The most critically
balanced and informative essay is David Hayman's "Balancing
the Book or Pro and Contra the Gabler *'Ulysses'*". This
collection can be considered as the reactionary response to the
Gabler edition, and as such, provides the grounds for debate
over the radically textual revision that has been favourably
received by other Joyce scholars.

Articles and Chapters in Books

I62   Larbaud, Valéry
        "The *Ulysses* of James Joyce", *Criterion*, 1 (1922), 94–103

        The earliest and one of the most perceptive critics of *Ulysses*
        was Valéry Larbaud, the Frenchman and friend of Joyce, who
        delivered a lecture on *Ulysses* in December 1921 when only
        half of the book had appeared serially. A fuller study by
        Larbaud was translated as "The *Ulysses* of James Joyce".
        Armed with Joyce's schema, Larbaud emphasizes the Homeric
        parallels and the symbolic patterns and concentrates on the
        central themes in the book.

I63   Pound, Ezra
        "James Joyce et Pécuchet" (1922), trans. Fred Bornhauser,
        Shenandoah, 3:3 (1952), 9–20

        Stresses Joyce's uncompromising realism which emanated out
        of the tradition of Flaubert but went beyond; Pound also
        insists on the unity of the work and compares it in form to the
        sonata. Although Pound places *Ulysses* in the tradition of
        Flaubert and realism, he uses the term "realism" in his own

special way. He praises the "luminous detail" that created the universal in the sharp and clearly focused particular, which in turn yielded a resonance beyond itself. He dismisses the Homeric structure as mere scaffolding and glosses over the more elaborate labyrinthian designs of the later chapters to concentrate on the "realism", the style, the counterpoint, the rhythm—those aspects of the work that emphasized its precision of detail. This essay established one important and persistent theme in *Ulysses* criticism with its emphasis on realism, a direction which provides a counterpoint to the mythic and symbolic elements first stressed by Eliot in his early essay *"Ulysses,* Order, and Myth". (Reprinted in the orginal French in B27.)

I64   Eliot, T. S.
"Ulysses, Order, and Myth", *Dial,* 75 (1923), 480–3

Reflects not only Eliot's appreciation and understanding of *Ulysses* but also his own critical and creative preoccupations. As with *The Waste Land,* he sees *Ulysses* as an attempt to come to terms with and create a synthesis out of what he regards as the chaos of the fragmented modern experience. He concentrates on what he sees as the central unifying method, the parallel to the *Odyssey,* which gave the book its shape and significance as it delicately balanced "contemporaneity and antiquity". While Pound stresses the work's inclusive realism, Eliot points out the classical dimensions, the deft parallels between the past and present, as well as the symbolist techniques and Joyce's use of myth, which provided a new method for giving shape to the "immense panorama of futility which is contemporary history". Although there is much in this essay with which to disagree, and Eliot later recanted several of his more extreme judgements, it remains the most influential single essay and set the critical groundwork for many studies that followed it. (Reprinted in D6 and D108.)

I65   Lewis, Wyndham
"An Analysis of the Mind of James Joyce", *Time and Western Man* (London: Chatto and Windus, 1927), pp. 91–130

An attack on the formlessness of *Ulysses,* calling it a "nightmare of the naturalistic method". Whether in spite of or because of his bombastic rhetoric and petulant imagery, he scores many points, accusing Joyce, among other things, of having "unorganized susceptibility to influences".

166   Curtius, Ernst Robert
"Technique and Thematic Development of James Joyce",
trans. Eugene Jolas, *transition*, 16–17 (1929), 310–25

Curtius' essay foreshadows in part the argument that was to be
developed by Stuart Gilbert a few years later. (See I2.)

167   Damon, S. Foster
"The Odyssey in Dublin; with a Postscript, 1947" (1929);
JAMES JOYCE: TWO DECADES OF CRITICISM, ed.
Seon Givens (1948; rev. edn, New York: Vanguard Press,
1963), pp. 203–42

An early essay which offered a broad assessment of the total
meaning of the work. The novel, according to Damon,
operated on three levels: the symbolic *(Odyssey)*, the spiritual
(The Divine Comedy), and the psychological *(Hamlet)*.
Homer offered the plot, Dante the setting, and Shakespeare
the motivation; the three major characters play out symbolic
roles, all of which culminate in the frustration and degradation
of the modern world. It is difficult to assess the influence of
Damon's allegorical reading, but the depth of his treatment of
the major themes and literary influences obviously opened up
further considerations for subsequent investigation. (Reprinted in D42.)

168   Wilson, Edmund L.
"James Joyce", AXEL'S CASTLE: A STUDY OF THE
IMAGINATIVE LITERATURE OF 1870–1930 (New York:
Scribner's, 1931), pp. 191–236

Wilson's discussion of *Ulysses* brings together the two
positions that Pound and Eliot had chosen to emphasize.
Wilson points out the affinities of *Ulysses* with both the
French naturalism of Flaubert and the French Symbolists and
shows how *Ulysses* joined the two. This is an important early
assessment of *Ulysses*, marked by its generous sympathies for
developments in modern literature and its broad understand-
ings of the aims of modernism.

I69   Beach, Joseph Warren
        "Post-Impressionism: Joyce", THE TWENTIETH-
        CENTURY NOVEL: STUDIES IN TECHNIQUE (New
        York: Appleton, 1932), pp. 403–24

        Emphasizes Joyce's technical accomplishments while placing
        Ulysses in the context of the modern novel.

I70   Jung, Carl G.
        "*Ulysses:* A Monologue" (1932), THE SPIRIT OF MAN,
        ART, AND LITERATURE, trans. R. F. C. Hull (Princeton:
        Princeton University Press, 1966), pp. 109–34

        Describes *Ulysses* as a cubistic work which, through its hidden
        rational control, depicted a world of seeming madness that
        revealed a new consciousness, "the epitome of being and not
        being", Jung's essay, although it frequently misses Joyce's
        point, is representative of the growing awareness among
        European intellectuals of the achievement of *Ulysses*.

I71   Troy, William
        "Stephen Dedalus and James Joyce", *Nation*, 138 (1934),
        187–8

        Sounds an early cautionary note against confusing the
        problematical and distasteful character of Stephen Dedalus
        with Joyce as a way of stressing that *Ulysses* is a work of great
        social importance. He also attacks his contemporary critics,
        especially the Marxists, whom he believes fail to understand
        the purpose of Joyce's art.

I72   More, Paul Elmer
        "James Joyce", ON BEING HUMAN (Princeton: Princeton
        University Press, 1936), pp. 69–96

        A noted humanist critic, More admires Joyce's linguistic and
        technical mastery but feels his achievement was limited by his
        rejection of an elevating philosophy.

I73   West, Alick
        "James Joyce: *Ulysses*" (1937), CRISIS AND CRITICISM
        AND SELECTED LITERARY ESSAYS (London:
        Lawrence and Wishart, 1975), pp. 143–80

Offers a perceptive social reading of the novel. One of the first
critics to bring out this aspect of Joyce's work.

I74   Frank, Joseph
       "Spatial Form in Modern Literature" (1945), THE
       WIDENING GYRE: CRISIS AND MASTERY IN
       MODERN LITERATURE (New Brunswick, N.J.: Rutgers
       University Press, 1963), pp. 3–62

       In a book which applies the aesthetic theory of Lessing to
       modern literature, Joyce is treated as part of a literary
       phenomenon which sought to create the illusion of spatial,
       three-dimensional form through the recognizable description
       of natural objects. A strong essay with forceful critical
       arguments.

I75   Blackmur, R. P.
       "The Jew in Search of a Son: Joyce's *Ulyssess*" (1948),
       ELEVEN ESSAYS IN THE EUROPEAN NOVEL (New
       York: Harcourt, 1964), pp. 27–47

       Brilliant essay on the paternity theme in *Ulysses* that depicts
       moral and cultural breakdown as the seminal theme in the
       novel, exemplified by the son's unfulfilled quest for the father.
       Explores Bloom's character in light of the individual's relation
       to society and the broad aesthetic question of the accessibility
       of *Ulysses* to the modern reader.

I76   Toynbee, Philip
       "A Study of James Joyce's *Ulysses*", JAMES JOYCE: TWO
       DECADES OF CRITICISM, ed. Seon Givens (1948: rev.
       edn, New York: Vanguard Press, 1963), pp. 243–84

       Exuberant in his support of *Ulysses* and points out the
       growing difference in method and purpose between the first
       half of the book and the second, taking into account the
       function of the imitative style in the later chapters.

I77   Heine, Arthur
       "Shakespeare in James Joyce", *Shakespeare Association
       Bulletin*, 24 (1949), 56–70

       Deals with Shakespearean elements in *Ulysses*.

I78   Duncan, Edward
       "Unsubstantial Father: A Study of the *Hamlet* Symbolism in
       Joyce's *Ulysses*", *University of Toronto Quarterly*, 19 (1950),
       126–40

       Useful for its outline of Stephen's theory of *Hamlet* as an
       autobiographical gloss on Shakespeare's life. After an attempt
       to apply this theory to Stephen's own troubled family
       relations, the author shifts emphasis from a paternal to a
       maternal conflict in both Shakespeare and Stephen but does
       not draw any specific conclusions.

I79   Savage, Derek S.
       "James Joyce", THE WITHERED BRANCH: SIX
       STUDIES IN THE MODERN NOVEL (London: Eyre and
       Spottiswoode, 1950), pp. 156–99

       Echoes Blackmur's view in that he saw no stability of values in
       the novel, no solidity of focus in a world of flux.

I80   Humphrey, Robert
       "Joyce's Daedal Network", STREAM OF
       CONSCIOUSNESS IN THE MODERN NOVEL (Berkeley
       and Los Angeles: University of California Press, 1954), pp.
       87–99

       Examines in part the stream-of-consciousness technique in
       Ulysses. The author presents seven categories of structure for
       stream-of-consciousness narrative in the modern novel and
       proceeds to discuss how Joyce incorporates them all.

I81   Friedman, Melvin J.
       "James Joyce: The Full Development of the Method",
       STREAM OF CONSCIOUSNESS: A STUDY OF
       LITERARY METHOD (New Haven: Yale University Press,
       1955), pp. 210–43

       Provides a brief history of Joyce's developing stream-of-
       consciousness technique from his early works to *Finnegans
       Wake*. The most valuable part of the chapter is the author's
       analysis of *Ulysses* as a casebook for the techniques of interior
       monologue. Each episode in the book is seen as applying a
       monologue of differing substance and rhythm in order to

distinguish the interior states of one character from another. *Finnegans Wake* is treated as a fanciful exaggeration of stream-of-consciousness.

I82   Empson, William
       "The Theme of *Ulysses*", *Kenyon Review*, 18 (1956), 26–52

       Empson's argument is a novel one, suggesting that Bloom attempts to get rid of Molly's current lover, Blazes Boylan, by substituting Stephen. It is a very different way of looking at *Ulysses*, and curiously enough, it accounts for certain aspects of the plot that many more plausible readings do not. (Reprinted with revisions in D23.)

I83   Cope, Jackson I.
       "The Rhythmic Gesture: Image and Aesthetic in Joyce's *Ulysses*", *ELH*, 29 (1962), 67–89

       Explores through examples from *Ulysses* the rhythmic aesthetics of Joyce, which associates a verbal gesture with the controlled expression of emotion.

I84   Gill, Richard
       "The 'Corporal Works of Mercy' as a Moral Pattern in Joyce's *Ulysses*", *Twentieth Century Literature*, 9:1 (1963), 17–21

       Investigates Bloom the Jew's performance of the Christian corporal works of mercy.

I85   Morse, J. Mitchell
       "Karl Gutzkow and the Novel of Simultaneity", *James Joyce Quarterly* 2:1 (Fall 1964), 13–17

       Offers a central position on Bloom's character, asserting that Bloom is among other things neurotic, naive and foolish, but also kind, good, brave and magnanimous.

I86   Boyle, Robert, S. J.
       "*Ulysses* as Frustrated Sonata Form", *James Joyce Quarterly*, 2:4 (Summer 1965), pp. 247–54

Boyle shares the results of his several years of teaching *Ulysses* as a sonata form, concluding that, at best, *Ulysses* is not an approximation of that form, nor was it intended to be.

I87   Tracy, Robert
        "Leopold Bloom Fourfold: A Hungarian–Hebraic–Hellenic–Hibernian Hero", *Massachusetts Review,* 6:3 (1965) 523–38

        Analysis of Bloom's ancestral characteristics.

I88   Kaplan, Harold
        "Stoom: the Universal Comedy of James Joyce", THE PASSIVE VOICE: AN APPROACH TO MODERN FICTION (Athens, Ohio: Ohio University Press, 1966), pp. 43–91

        After a brief summary of mock-priestly elements in Joyce's early fiction, the author investigates in a very general manner the comic and parodic effects in *Ulysses*. The author concludes that Stephen represents a great intellectual comedy, Bloom the physical and social comedy, and that together they combine to produce a universal comic vision.

I89   Bauerle, Ruth
        "A Sober Drunken Speech: Stephen's Parodies in 'The Oxen of the Sun'", *James Joyce Quarterly*, 5:1 (Fall 1967), 40–6

        Discusses Stephen's parodies of liturgical and religious documents and services.

I90   Hayman, David
        "Forms of Folly in Joyce: A Study of Clowning in *Ulysses*", *ELH*, 34 (1967), 260–83

        The fullest and most interesting discussion of the comic elements in *Ulysses*.

I91   Praz, Mario
        "James Joyce", JAMES JOYCE, THOMAS STEARNS ELIOT: DUE MAESTRI DEI MODERNI (Turin: Edizioni Rai Radiotelevisione Italiana, 1967), pp. 3–82

A broad study enriched by a wealth of background on the two writers, but not a comparative examination.

I92   Herring, Phillip F.
"The Bedsteadfastness of Molly Bloom", *Modern Fiction Studies*, 15 (1969), pp. 49–61

Suggests that a more balanced reading of Molly can be obtained by looking at her characterization in the broader terms of Joyce's artistic aims. His essay also provides a sound summary of previous criticism on Molly: Budgen, Gilbert, Ellmann, Kain, Prescott and Tindall find her "in varying degrees attractive"; Kenner's early view (*Dublin's Joyce*) is negative; Goldberg scores the "emotional falsity"; and other critics find her gross, repulsive, lascivious. Herring's essay point out the polarity of critical opinion and the nature of its divergence.

I93   Allott, Miriam
"James Joyce: The Hedgehog and the Fox", ON THE NOVEL: A PRESENT FOR WALTER ALLEN ON HIS 60TH BIRTHDAY FROM HIS FRIENDS, ed. B. S. Benedikz (London: Dent, 1971), pp. 161–77

Concludes "the true and strong things in *Ulysses* derive from the qualities celebrated in Leopold Bloom, the man who watches 'kindly and curiously' everything from his cat to his Penelope; who reflects on everything, feels something for all he sees, is sensuous, observant and weak, rarely impatient, and always generous."

I94   Card, James Van Dyck
"A Gibraltar Sourcebook of 'Penelope'", *James Joyce Quarterly* 8:2 (Winter 1971), 163–75

Begins with a discussion of Joyce's notesheets used in revising *Ulysses* and proceeds to compare these notes to a source book for the "Penelope" chapter, Henry M. Field's *Gibraltar*. This comparison is used as a basis for demonstrating the selectivity and organization of Joyce's creative process.

I95   Day, Robert Adams
"Joyce's Waste Land and Eliot's Unknown God", *Literary*

Monographs, vol. 4, ed. Eric Rothstein (Madison: University of Wisconsin Press, 1971), pp. 139–210; 218–26

The most exhaustive study of the influence of *Ulysses* on *The Waste Land*. A thorough and careful analysis.

I96   Fiedler, Leslie
"Bloom on Joyce: or, Jokey for Jacob", NEW LIGHT ON JOYCE FROM THE DUBLIN SYMPOSIUM, ed. Fritz Senn (Bloomington: Indiana University Press, 1972), pp. 195–208

Praises Bloom extravagantly: "Bloom is not merely mythic, much less an ironic commentary on a dying myth. He is a true, a full myth, a new and living myth."

I97   Hyman, Louis
"Some Aspects of the Jewish Background of *Ulysses*", THE JEWS OF IRELAND: FROM THE EARLIEST TIMES TO THE YEAR 1910 (Shannon: Irish University Press, 1972), pp. 167–92

Examines, among other things, genealogical evidence of the surname Bloom in Ireland and also explores the relations between the Irish and Jews in turn-of-the-century Dublin.

I98   Iser, Wolfgang
"Patterns of Communication in Joyce's *Ulysses*", THE IMPLIED READER: PATTERNS OF COMMUNICATION IN PROSE FICTION FROM BUNYAN TO BECKETT (Baltimore: Johns Hopkins University Press, 1974), pp. 196–233

From the loosely collective position of the Konstanz School, Iser is a theorist known as a "reader-response" critic. He applies these methods to *Ulysses* with quite interesting results. In these pages he is especially concerned with the experimental style of *Ulysses*.

I99   Litz, A. Walton
"The Genre of *Ulysses*", THE THEORY OF THE NOVEL, ed. John Halperin (New York: Oxford University Press, 1974), pp. 109–120

Argues in detail points raised by Goldberg's *The Classical Temper*, but Litz's essay is important beyond its argument with Goldberg, for he reviews theoretical attempts to define the genre of *Ulysses*, a problem with which many critics have attempted to come to terms. The work stands, as Litz points out, "at the confluence of so many literary traditions and genres ... that it has become the supreme challenge for the theoretical critic of fiction".

I100   Kimpel, Ben D.
"The Voices of *Ulysses*", *Style,* 9 (1975), pp. 283–319

Argues that the critical preoccupation with stream-of-consciousness has prevented an appreciation of the later chapters of *Ulysses*, which are based on a multiplicity of narrative voices. The author also defends Joyce's creation of manifold styles, not as sterile technical demonstration, but as an integral part of the novel.

I101   Moss, Roger
"Difficult Language: The Justification of Joyce's Syntax in *Ulysses*", THE MODERN ENGLISH NOVEL: THE READER, THE WRITER AND THE WORK, ed. Gabriel Josipovici (London: Open Books Publishing, 1976; New York: Barnes and Noble, 1976), pp. 130–48

Discussion on the subject of style and syntax as reinforcement of the major tension in the novel between freedom and order.

I102   Niemeyer, Carl
"A *Ulysses* Calendar", *James Joyce Quarterly,* 13:2 (Winter 1976), 163–93

Disregards the implications of Joyce's carefully worked-out system of realistic chronology, instead concentrating on the wealth of inadvertent calendrical errors which by the very nature of their casual inconsistency build additional layers of meaning into the text.

I103   Cohn, Dorrit
TRANSPARENT MINDS: NARRATIVE MODES FOR PRESENTING CONSCIOUSNESS IN FICTION

(Princeton: Princeton University Press, 1978), pp. 82–8; 91–8; 217–34 and passim

This book as a whole differentiates patterns in the language of fiction from the statement language of reality. The author examines a variety of interior monologue devices and devotes a section to "Penelope", as a means of establishing the essentially anti-realistic aspect of psychological narration.

I104   Gaskell, Philip
       "Joyce, *Ulysses*, 1922", FROM WRITER TO READER: STUDIES IN EDITORIAL METHOD (New York: Oxford University Press, 1978), pp. 213–44

A brief account of the complex textual history of *Ulysses* that outlines the editorial problems of producing a corrected text. For illustrative purposes, the author presents the surviving textual states that led up to page 153 of "Lestrygonians". This essay is an interesting forecast of the editorial efforts in progress which eventually produced the synoptic edition of *Ulysses* and the *James Joyce Archives*.

I105   Herring, Phillip F.
       "Toward an Historical Molly Bloom", *ELH*, 45 (1978), pp. 501–21

Constructs a surmised historical and sociological background for Molly Bloom based on the narrative fact that she is a lady from Gibraltar. Using guidebooks and journalistic and literary sources that Joyce read, Herring speculates on the thoughts of "an historical Molly Bloom" which result in her leaving Gibraltar.

I106   Iser, Wolfgang
       THE ACT OF READING: A THEORY OF AESTHETIC RESPONSE (Baltimore: Johns Hopkins University Press, 1978), pp. 207–11 and passim

A theoretical study in reader-response criticisms, which includes discussion of *Ulysses* from this critical perspective.

I107   McBride, Margaret
        "At Four She Said", *James Joyce Quarterly*, 17:1 (Fall,
        1979), 21–39; 18–4 (Summer 1981), 417–31

        These two pieces argue that Bloom suffers a time fixation
        based on verbal repression of information he subconsciously
        knows. This complex comes to a traumatic focal point at the
        hour of Boylan's assignation with Molly.

I108   Spilka, Mark
        "Leopold Bloom as Jewish Pickwick: A Neo-Dickensian
        Perspective", *Novel*, 13 (Fall 1979), pp. 121–46

        It includes the fine perception that as sex was a taboo for
        nineteenth-century Dickens, so sentimentality was for
        twentieth-century James Joyce.

I109   Robinson, Fred Miller
        "Joyce: *Ulysses*", THE COMEDY OF LANGUAGE:
        STUDIES IN MODERN COMIC LITERATURE
        (Amherst: University of Massachusetts Press, 1980), pp.
        25–50

        Argues that comedies of language are the essential texts in the
        study of modern comedy. His theory of comedy, which is
        especially revealing when applied to modern works such as
        Ulysses, is based on the contradiction between the descriptive
        capacity of language and the nature of reality as metaphysical
        flux. Robinson says that *Ulysses* is strengthened by this
        contradiction and calls the book, along with other modern
        works, a comedy of language. His chapter on *Ulysses* both
        supports his theory and reveals how Joyce worked in this
        mode.

I110   Gabler, Hans Walter
        "The Synchrony and Diachrony of Texts: Practice and
        Theory of the Critical Edition of James Joyce's *Ulysses*",
        TEXT: TRANSACTIONS OF THE SOCIETY FOR
        TEXTUAL SCHOLARSHIP (New York: AMS Press, 1981),
        305–26

        Gabler explains succinctly the editorial theory that informed
        his reconstruction of the *Ulysses* text. He proposes that a

literary work should not be viewed in isolation from the historical (or diachronic) data of its composition. Gabler urges that critical interpretation take into account a combination of authorial revisions and corrected errors of pre-publication transmission in order to establish a richer reading of the text. This essay provides the theoretical justification for the controversial textual revision of the Gabler *Ulysses* which appeared in 1984.

I111   Burgan, Mary
"Androgynous Fatherhood in *Ulysses* and *Women in Love*", *Modern Language Quarterly*, 44:2 (June 1983), 178–197

Explores the different ways in which Joyce and Lawrence sought to express the ideal of an androgynous fatherhood. Both authors are seen as viewing the feminine negatively in terms of restrictive motherly influence and conventional images of maternal passivity, yet positively as a passionate usurpation of feminine qualities which serve as models of creativity.

I112   Engel, Monroe
"Contrived Lives: Joyce and Lawrence", MODERNISM RECONSIDERED, eds Robert Kiely and John Hildebidle (Cambridge, Mass.: Harvard University Press, 1983), pp. 65–80

Argues that Joyce and Lawrence are the two great monogamous imaginations of the modern age. Both insisted on a monogamy in their writings, characterized by tension, disappointment and betrayal, but which provided a person's only defence against the greater inadequacies of the world.

I113   Heusel, Barbara Stevens
"Parallax as a Metaphor for the Structure of *Ulysses*", *Studies in the Novel*, 15:2 (Summer 1983), 135–146

Examines aspects of parallactic structure in *Ulysses* as a way that Joyce showed the consequences of a divided vision, finally forcing the reader near the end of "Ithaca" to synthesize the two divergent, shifting perspectives of Bloom and Dedalus into a single stereoscopic vision.

I114 Fogel, Daniel Mark
"henryJAMESjoyce: The Succession of the Masters",
Journal of Modern Literature, 11:2 (July 1984), 199–229

Traces an extensive, covert network of allusions to Henry
James in *Ulysses* as a basis for the claim that the American
novelist should take his place beside Homer, Dante,
Shakespeare and Flaubert as major influences on Joyce's
work.

I115 Kenner, Hugh
"Who's He When He's at Home?", LIGHT RAYS: JAMES
JOYCE AND MODERNISM, ed. Heyward Ehrlich (New
York: New Horizon, 1984), pp. 58–69

An investigation into the complex question of identity,
stressing the constant renaming of characters. Kenner suggests
that characterization in the book is made up of metamorphoses, reincarnations and impersonations, part of which
are created by authorial design and the rest by the text itself.

I116 Lees, Heath
"The Introduction to 'Sirens' and the *Fuga per Canonem*",
James Joyce Quarterly 22:1 (Fall 1984), 39–54

Takes issue with the viewpoint that the opening of "Sirens" is
meaningless as a loose collection of musical motifs. Heath
analyses this section as strictly conforming to the principles of
a *fuga per canonem*, as Joyce suggested should be done,
specifically Bach's *The Art of Fugue*.

I117 Martin, Augustine
"Novelist and City: The Technical Challenge", THE IRISH
WRITER AND THE CITY, ed. Maurice Harmon (Gerrards
Cross, Buckinghamshire: Smythe, 1984; Totowa, N.J.: Barnes
and Noble, 1984), pp. 37–51

This essay explores how Joyce devised a technique that
embodied the complex drama of a city's life, the Dublin of
Ulysses, without relying on the distracting structure of a
traditional plot. It is this technical accomplishment that
distinguishes Joyce from previous novelists of the city such as
Dickens, Balzac and Zola.

Finnegans Wake

Books

J1   Beckett, Samuel, *et al.*
      OUR EXAGMINATION ROUND HIS FACTIFICATION
      FOR INCAMINATION OF "WORK IN PROGRESS"
      (Paris: Shakespeare and Co., 1929; rpt 1974)

Offers a preliminary understanding of Joyce's purposes. The
book, orchestrated by Joyce himself, has a bit of the publicity
release about it, or so it seems in retrospect, but such a notion
does not diminish the importance of this volume which
includes contributions by several important contemporaries of
Joyce. Although Beckett's essay, "Dante ... Bruno. Vico ...
Joyce", has been given the most attention, Frank Budgen's
"James Joyce's 'Work in Progress' and Old Norse Poetry" is
the best in the volume. Also, Robert McAlmon offers several
good observations on the language ("Mr. Joyce Directs an
Irish Word Ballet"), and William Carlos Williams provides a
sharp view of the modernist literary background ("A Point for
American Criticism").

J2   Campbell, Joseph, and Henry Morton Robinson
      A SKELETON KEY TO "*FINNEGANS WAKE*" (New
      York: Harcourt, 1944; London: Faber and Faber, 1947)

A highly influential work, but one which hardly unlocked the
secrets of the book. The authors' accomplishment cannot be
undervalued in spite of the many errors in the book and its
undue emphasis on the mythic aspects of *Finnegans Wake*,
which led them to see the work as largely allegorical. The
authors of the *Key* attempted to offer a translation of the
book, or to provide a summary, but their resulting emphasis
on the mythic level, the cycles of human development, and the
racial unconscious presented a severely unbalanced reading.

J3   Glasheen, Adaline
      A CENSUS OF *FINNEGANS WAKE*: AN INDEX OF
      THE CHARACTERS AND THEIR ROLES (Evanston,
      Ill.: Northwestern University Press, 1956; London: Faber
      and Faber, 1957); A SECOND CENSUS OF *FINNEGANS
      WAKE*: AN INDEX OF THE CHARACTERS AND
      THEIR ROLES (Evanston, Ill.: Northwestern University
      Press, 1963); and A THIRD CENSUS OF *FINNEGANS
      WAKE*: AN INDEX OF THE CHARACTERS AND
      THEIR ROLES (Berkeley and Los Angeles: University of
      California Press, 1977)

      A Census of "Finnegans Wake" (1956) and *A Second Census
      of "Finnegans Wake"* (1963) represented a new direction in
      Wake studies—away from the broad interpretations to closer
      analysis of content and an application of empirical methods.
      The *Third Census*, superseding the previous two, greatly
      amplifies the list of personal names and the other litter of the
      "divine and human comedy", and although the author
      modestly claims that even this *Third Census* is an interim
      report, it is of enormous value to the student of the *Wake*.
      Glasheen's revised synopsis in the 1977 edition is more detailed
      than her earlier ones, and her chart "Who is Who When
      Everybody is Somebody Else" is extremely helpful in putting
      the almost hopelessly variegated connections in some kind of
      order. To use her own words in a different context, Glasheen is
      the archaeologist and augur who reads the signs of the *Wake*
      as well as anyone.

J4   Atherton, James S.
      THE BOOKS AT THE WAKE: A STUDY OF LITERARY
      ALLUSIONS IN JAMES JOYCE'S *FINNEGANS WAKE*
      (London: Faber and Faber, 1959; New York: Viking, 1960;
      rpt 1974)

      Divided into three parts—the structural books, the literary
      sources and the sacred books—Atherton's work offers a
      careful scrutiny of the multilevel structures and patterns of
      Finnegans Wake and a penetrating analysis of Joyce's richly
      allusive method. In the reprinting of *Books at the Wake*,
      Atherton has revised and enlarged the appendix of literary
      allusions, adding three new discoveries and deleting several
      entries from the first edition.

J5   Boldereff, Frances M.
        READING *FINNEGANS WAKE* (New York: Barnes and
        Noble, 1959)

        This book is of some value for its noting of Irish allusions and
        certain curious and arcane observations. Yet Boldereff's study
        (along with her later *Hermes to His Son Thoth: Being Joyce's
        Use of Giordano Bruno in "Finnegans Wake"*) represents
        several of the worst aspects of literary criticism; whatever
        intelligent comment is present is wholly lost by excessive,
        fallacious and extravagant claims pulled wildly from the
        imagination without critical principle or analysis. These works
        deserve mention because they represent a small but persistent
        fringe that has existed in the response to the *Wake*.

J6   Connolly, Thomas E., ed.
        SCRIBBLEDEHOBBLE: THE UR-WORKBOOK FOR
        FINNEGANS WAKE (Evanston, Ill.: Northwestern
        University Press, 1961)

        A transcription of a notebook written in Joyce's hand that
        relates to the early history of *Finnegans Wake*. The accuracy
        in transcribing the document, however, was far from
        convincing and even a subsequent publication of a list of
        errata by David Hayman (*James Joyce Quarterly*, 1:2, Winter
        1964, 23–9) has not enhanced the work's usefulness.

J7   Hart, Clive
        STRUCTURE AND MOTIF IN *FINNEGANS WAKE*
        (Evanston, Ill.: Northwestern University Press, 1962)

        Offers an analysis of the broad architectonics of *Finnegans
        Wake* and describes in careful detail the correspondences and
        the complex formal patterns, the major ordering principles.
        Hart concentrates on the spatial configurations he believes
        Joyce had in mind as he conceptualized and wrote the book,
        and which provide the structural tensions for it. Hart's study
        may appear overly schematic, but, nevertheless, he acutely
        explores the organic structure of *Finnegans Wake* and the way
        the formal beauty enriches, expands, and deepens the
        individual sections and passages and provides a richly textured
        meaning. In this balanced study the characters are never lost
        but are better understood, and their roles as well as their
        individuality are made more clear. Hart's work will remain an
        important and pivotal study in *Wake* scholarship.

J8   Benstock, Bernard
JOYCE-AGAIN'S WAKE: AN ANALYSIS OF
FINNEGANS WAKE (Seattle: University of Washington
Press, 1965)

An attempt to bridge the specialized works that appeared
previously, this book is designed for "middle-range" readers—
"those with enough patience to be willing to participate in the
work necessary for an understanding of Joyce's masterpiece,
but without that ideal insomnia being simulated by Joycean
scholars". Benstock begins with a working outline of the book
and then offers an excellent discussion of Joyce's religious and
political background. In subsequent chapters he discusses the
narrative, comic and epic elements in *Finnegans Wake*.
Animated by a lucid and enthusiastic style, with an eye for
excellent textual examples to clarify points, this work does
narrow the gap between specialist and non-specialist. For the
non-specialist it opens up doors to understanding because he
deals with the *Wake* as a work of literature, and Benstock's
critical method is easily discernible and amply fulfilled in his
analysis.

J9   Christiani, Dounia Bunis
SCANDINAVIAN ELEMENTS OF *FINNEGANS WAKE*
(Evanston, Ill.: Northwestern University Press, 1965)

Provides basic linguistic background and offers detailed
comment as well as translations, but it lacks a coherent
methodology and reflects a number of serious misreadings.

J10   Dalton, Jack P., and Clive Hart, eds
TWELVE AND A TILLY: ESSAYS ON THE OCCASION
OF THE 25TH ANNIVERSARY OF *FINNEGANS WAKE*
(Evanston, Ill.: Northwestern University Press, 1965 [1966])

Essays by well-known Joyce scholars. Frank Budgen, Richard
M. Kain, Frederick J. Hoffman and Vivian Mercier offer
general essays. A. Walton Litz suggests the uses to be made of
the *Wake* manuscripts, and Dalton discussses the text; the
remaining essays are of a more specialized nature, dealing with
narrower aspects of the book.

J11   *"Finnegans Wake* Issue", *James Joyce Quarterly*, 2:3 (Spring
1965), 141–236

This issue, edited by David Hayman, presents various topics on the *Wake*. J. S. Atherton adds to his already extensive studies of literary allusions; Dounia Christiani reviews the actual historical roles of the Vikings and their place in Irish history; Brendan O'Hehir looks at the multitudinous references to Anna Livia which suggest Gaelic roots, especially proper names and places; Hugh Staples explores Joyce's interest in cryptology, specifically the acrostic, the anagram and the cryptogram; Ronald Bates argues that *Finnegans Wake* takes place during the same year as *Ulysses*; Bernard Benstock compiles a list of food references, and collects the addresses of principal characters; and David Hayman suggests that Joyce's night language derives in part from the eccentric style in the letters of Ezra Pound.

J12   Bonheim, Helmut
        A LEXICON OF THE GERMAN IN *FINNEGANS WAKE*
        (Berkeley and Los Angeles: University of California Press,
        1967)

        Provides basic linguistic background and a solid understand-
        ing of the book as a whole.

J13   O'Hehir, Brendan, comp.
        A GAELIC LEXICON FOR *FINNEGANS WAKE* AND
        GLOSSARY FOR JOYCE'S OTHER WORKS (Berkeley
        and Los Angeles: University of California Press, 1967)

        Provides basic linguistic background.

J14   Hart, Clive, and Fritz Senn, eds
        A *WAKE* DIGEST (Sydney: Sydney University Press, 1968;
        University Park: Pennsylvania State Press, 1968; London:
        Methuen, 1968)

        A collection of brief essays and notes which discuss matters of
        general explication, source studies and linguistics. Most of
        these pieces have already appeared in *A Wake Newslitter*
        edited by the same authors, and this volume contains a
        selection of the best, including Clive Hart's essay on exegetical
        guidelines for the *Wake*, "The Elephant in the Belly: Exegesis
        of *Finnegans Wake*". Hart's piece sets out six propositions or
        guidelines concerning the reading and exegesis of *Finnegans*

Wake—principles of explication which would avoid speculative excesses, yet, at the same time, not be bound by an all-too-rigorous rational and logical method that would lead to an expulsion of the poetry of the work. This carefully reasoned essay, though frequently debated among *Wake* scholars, has been an important influence.

J15   Solomon, Margaret C.
ETERNAL GEOMATER: THE SEXUAL UNIVERSE OF
FINNEGANS WAKE (Carbondale: Southern Illinois
University Press, 1969)

The first extended study to deal with a single thematic aspect of the book. Solomon looks at sexual themes and representations in a number of sections of the *Wake* specifically as they relate to geometric forms. It is clearly aimed at the specialist, for it assumes a close familiarity with the text. Although difficult to follow at times, it is an illuminating study and is especially valuable for its treatment of a number of geometrical forms such as the circle. The thesis developed regarding Joyce's geometrics, however, is somewhat forced; later critics have extended a number of Solomon's propositions profitably.

J16   Tindall, William York
A READER'S GUIDE TO *FINNEGANS WAKE* (New
York: Farrar, Straus and Giroux, 1969)

Although frequently insightful, is limited in scope, presenting a running commentary on selected words and paragraphs that, in the opinion of the author, are essential for a basic grasp of the book. This work, however, continued the trend of closer readings of the text and explicated a number of seemingly obscure passages.

J17   "Finnegans Wake Issue", *James Joyce Quarterly*, 9:2 (Winter
1972), 124–269

Another *Finnegans Wake* special issue of *James Joyce Quarterly*. Grace Eckley discusses various aspects of the Prankquean episode; Arthur T. Broes provides source materials; James W. Cerny investigates the river names imbedded in the *Wake*; W. V. Costanzo discusses Joyce's

participation in the French translation of the *Wake*; Ronald J.
Koch analyses a short paragraph as a basis for examining the
influence on Joyce of Giordano Bruno; Kevin McCarthy notes
Turkish references; and Timothy Ransom discusses the
analogy between a ringing bell and Joyce's complex verbal
sonorities.

J18   Jacquet, Claude
       JOYCE ET RABELAIS: ASPECTS DE LA CRÉATION
       VERBALE DANS *FINNEGANS WAKE* (Paris: M. Didier,
       1972)

       A valuable study which provides an answer to the difficulty of
       determining the extent of Joyce's knowledge of an author or
       group of authors. Joyce himself pointed to this problem when
       he wrote to Harriet Weaver in 1927, "I never read Rabelais
       even though nobody will believe this ... I read a few chapters
       of a book called *La Langue de Rabelais*." Jacquet collates
       Joyce's Buffalo notebook VI.B.42 with Sainean's *La Langue
       de Rabelais* and shows how this work contributed to Joyce's
       verbal construction in the *Wake*.

J19   Begnal, Michael H., and Fritz Senn, eds
       A CONCEPTUAL GUIDE TO *FINNEGANS WAKE*
       (University Park: Pennsylvania State University Press, 1974)

       Suggests a systematic approach. Although this work does
       attempt to cover all the books and chapters of *Finnegans
       Wake*, the unity and coverage for which the editors aimed are
       not offered. Begnal notes in his introduction that it is not the
       purpose of the volume to provide a new collective paraphrase,
       but to offer "entry into a section at something deeper than a
       surface level". Frequently insightful as they are, very few of the
       essays offer sufficiently broad coverage of the books or
       chapters of the *Wake* that they deal with. For example, J.
       Mitchell Morse's essay is largely a treatment of Vico and does
       not pretend to cover the first chapter as a whole. Roland
       McHugh does cover Chapters 2–4 of Book I and discusses the
       attacks on Earwicker, his trial and entombment. Benstock and
       Epstein follow with good coverage of Chapters 5 and 6.
       Boyle's essay on Chapter 7 and 8 of Book I is far more narrow
       in its coverage and broader in its implication. Concentrating
       largely on pages 185–6 in Chapter 7, Boyle discussed Joyce's
       emerging artistic vision, culminating in the controlling
       metaphor in this passage and Joyce's debt to Oscar Wilde.

J20   "*Finnegans Wake* Issue", *James Joyce Quarterly*, 11:4
       (Summer 1974), 307–405

       Includes a number of notable essays. Leo Knuth, in
       "*Finnegans Wake*: A Product of the Twenties", speculates on
       how Joyce captured the spirit of uncertainty and doubt which
       pervaded the 1920s. He argues that in an age of specialists,
       coterie art does not necessarily mean a lack of relevance to the
       period in which it was written. Knuth's argument counters
       many of the contentions of earlier critics. David Hayman, in
       "Farcical Themes and Forms in *Finnegans Wake*", argues that
       most if not all situations in the *Wake* are farcical and that
       characters assume the role of clowns acting in various
       irreverent poses to unsettle and even frustrate the reader.
       Margot Norris gives essentially a structuralist-based study in
       her "The Function of Mythic Repetition in *Finnegans Wake*",
       and Eric McLuhan discussses structural motifs in "The
       Rhetorical Structure of *Finnegans Wake*".

J21   Begnal, Michael H., and Grace Eckley
       NARRATOR AND CHARACTER IN *FINNEGANS
       WAKE* (Lewisburg, Pa: Bucknell University Press, 1975)

       Begnal analyses the ironies of the *Wake* in his study of
       narration and point of view, which is actually a careful
       isolation of the separate speakers in the *Wake* to determine
       who is speaking. He contends that once the reader isolates the
       various characters and determines points of view, the book is
       not quite so complicated as previous critics have made out.
       Eckley analyses the "Anna Livia Plurabelle" chapter and sees
       it as the centre of the book.

J22   McHugh, Roland
       THE SIGLA OF *FINNEGANS WAKE* (Austin: University
       of Texas Press, 1976)

       Primarily exegetical, but his sigla approach substitutes ciphers
       for established terminology.

J23   Motz, Reighard
       TIME AS JOYCE TELLS IT (Mifflingburg, Pa: Mutford
       Colebrook, 1977)

A book of little note that comments on, among other diversions, what Motz concludes are time passages in the *Wake*.

J24   Norris, Margot C.
THE DECENTERED UNIVERSE OF *FINNEGANS WAKE*: A STRUCTURALIST ANALYSIS (Baltimore: Johns Hopkins University Press, 1977)

One of the first books on the *Wake* to make extensive use of the structuralist method, Norris is also indebted to psychoanalytic approaches to literature. For Norris the dislocated dream meanings produce a decentred universe in the *Wake*. The method in this study is extremely engaging as it moves away from interpretation as a single locus for *Wake* criticism.

J25   O'Hehir, Brendon, and John M. Dillon, comps
A CLASSICAL LEXICON FOR *FINNEGANS WAKE*: A GLOSSARY OF THE GREEK AND LATIN IN THE MAJOR WORKS OF JOYCE (Berkeley and Los Angeles: University of California Press, 1977)

Gives a glossary of the Greek and Latin in all of Joyce's work as well as in *Finnegans Wake*, and the appendices provide a more detailed explanation of Joyce's use of classical language.

J26   Drachler, Jacob
ID-GRIDS AND EGO-GRAPHS: A CONFABULATION WITH *FINNEGANS WAKE* (Brooklyn, N.Y.: Gridgraffiti Press, 1978)

A curious work. A suite of forty-four black-and-white mixed-media graphics described as "a confrontation with *Finnegans Wake*".

J27   Hayman, David, and Elliott Anderson, eds
IN THE WAKE OF THE *WAKE* (Madison: University of Wisconsin Press, 1978)

Contains essays responding to the *Wake* and pieces written in the spirit of the *Wake*. It would be simplistic and therefore rash to categorize the contributors to this volume, but all of them reflect either a post-modern orientation, as in the contributions by Samuel Beckett, John Cage, Raymond Federman and William Gass, or recent European theoretical concerns, as in the contributions by Philippe Sollers, Michael Finney and Hélène Cixous. The editors' introduction establishes an excellent context both for the *Wake* and for the contributions that follow. Finney's essay provides interesting commentary and background for "Work in Progress" as it appeared in Eugene Jolas' *transition*, especially in the light of Jolas' manifesto "Revolution of the Word" and other pronouncements that were running concurrently in *transition* with "Work in Progress". As Finney points out, Joyce surely only tolerated these views because Jolas was the editor and was publishing parts of the *Wake* in each issue.

J28   Mink, Louis O., ed.
A *FINNEGANS WAKE* GAZETTEER (Bloomington: Indiana University Press, 1978)

Gives 2,800 topographical identifications from the *Wake*, "topographical" referring not only to geographical allusions but also to words and phrases that have literary, biographical and historical overtones. The latter category is especially valuable for the Dublin references. We learn, too, that many places are not places as we had assumed but things that might have been named after places. The book is divided into two parts, a "Linear Guide" and an "Alphabetical Gazetteer". The second part is arranged according to the "plain-text" rubric in Part 1, and it includes a complete inventory of the same identifications numerically listed by page. Part 2 also includes four well-detailed maps. Mink prefaces this work of impeccable scholarship with a number of short introductions that discuss the patterns of topographical allusion in the *Wake*. Mink's book is indispensable to the serious study of *Finnegans Wake*.

J29   DiBernard, Barbara
ALCHEMY AND *FINNEGANS WAKE* (Albany: State University of New York Press, 1980)

A detailed study of alchemy and its various uses in the *Wake*. That Joyce was interested in the subject fairly early in his literary career has been discussed by critics as early as Stuart

Gilbert. DiBernard sees Joyce using alchemy as a metaphor for change and the artistic process, especially the idea of transmutation. This is a clear and well-developed study of a difficult and elusive subject.

J30   McCarthy, Patrick A.
THE RIDDLES OF *FINNEGANS WAKE* (Rutherford, N. J.: Fairleigh Dickinson University Press, 1980)

This study explores riddle consciousness in *Finnegans Wake*. Beginning with the psychological and social aspects of puzzles, the author examines the connection between riddle motifs and thematic concerns in Joyce. Much of the study is devoted to analysing the major riddles in the *Wake*: the quiz chapter, Prankquean's riddle, Izod's heliotrope, and Shem's first riddle of the universe. This book is noteworthy for its sophisticated yet clear analysis and its amusing style of presentation.

J31   McHugh, Roland
ANNOTATIONS TO *FINNEGANS WAKE* (Baltimore: Johns Hopkins University Press, 1980)

McHugh's compilation, as he readily notes in his preface, is the outgrowth of many years of exegetical study by Hart, Knuth, Senn and many others; it "attempts to cope with the formidable secondary task of identifying the components of the text by applying the cream of all available exegesis in as condensed and accessible form as possible." The form of McHugh's volume is a masterstroke, providing as it does a single numbered page for every numbered page of the *Wake*, with annotations appearing on the lines corresponding to those of the text of the *Wake*.

J32   McHugh, Roland
THE *FINNEGANS WAKE* EXPERIENCE (Dublin: Irish Academic Press, 1981; Berkeley and Los Angeles: University of California Press, 1981)

An attempt to introduce *Finnegans Wake* to beginning readers through elementary textual strategies and a discussion of manuscript and other archival evidence. It should be noted that McHugh treats the text as a technical system to be handled by lexical, bibliographical and archival tools. This approach may be limiting or even intimidating to a first-time reader of Joyce, yet anyone interested in a basically scientific rather than imaginative grasp of the *Wake* will profit from this book.

J33   Rose, Danis, and John O'Hanlon
UNDERSTANDING *FINNEGANS WAKE*: A GUIDE TO THE NARRATIVE OF JAMES JOYCE'S MASTERPIECE (New York and London: Garland, 1982)

A clear, straightforward narrative guide to *Finnegans Wake*, based on the authors' extensive familiarity with the manuscript and notebook materials Joyce used for composing the book. This interpretation relies on the theory that Joyce's art is not one of creative originality but rather a syncretic, mosaic method. Thus the *Wake* becomes a book of quotations, adaptations and transformations of previously-existing compositions. *Understanding Finnegans Wake* represents this "manuscript school" of Joyce criticism, and the authors seek to explicate and structure Joyce's complex final product in terms of the more simple constructions found in the archival evidence.

J34   White, David A.
THE GRAND CONTINUUM: REFLECTIONS ON JOYCE AND METAPHYSICS (Pittsburgh: University of Pittsburgh Press, 1983)

An examination of the metaphysical system of *Finnegans Wake* and its relevance to modern philosphy. The author suggests parallels between Joyce and Heidegger, Wittgenstein and Husserl, defining Joyce's metaphysics as process in flux with no fixed realities. White, however, restricts himself to modern metaphysical issues with no consideration for Joyce's main philosophical influences; medieval scholasticism, Bruno and Vico. Most valuable for its treatment of *Finnegans Wake* and for the connection provided between literature and philosophy in the modern age.

J35   Cheng, Vincent John
SHAKESPEARE AND JOYCE: A STUDY OF *FINNEGANS WAKE* (University Park and London: Pennsylvania State University Press, 1984)

An account of Shakespearean allusion in *Finnegans Wake*, this study is both an exegesis and a scholarly reference tool. Part I connects Shakespearean allusion to themes and characters in *Finnegans Wake*. Cheng compares entire plays such as *Hamlet* and *Finnegans Wake*, and also draws parallels between characters such as Laertes and Shaun and Ophelia and Issy. The second part contains explications of a thousand Shakespearean allusions in *Finnegans Wake*.

J36   Patell, Cyrus R. K.
JOYCE'S USE OF HISTORY IN *FINNEGANS WAKE*
(Cambridge: Harvard University Press, 1984)

Through a heavy emphasis on Viconian cycles, Patell examines Joyce's attempt in *Finnegans Wake* to capture human history as principally embodied in the language of an individual's unconscious states. Joyce is thus viewed as a preserver of stories about humanity. History is considered as a record of mental states dependent upon language.

J37   Eckley, Grace
CHILDREN'S LORE IN *FINNEGANS WAKE* (Syracuse: Syracuse University Press, 1985)

Written by a specialist in children's lore and literature, this book is especially useful in dealing with children's games, rituals and songs in *Finnegans Wake*. Outside this area the author speculates with only slender or questionable evidence: for example, she asserts that the character of H. C. Earwicker is based on the author and journalist William T. Stead.

J38   Bishop, John
JOYCE'S BOOK OF THE DARK: *FINNEGANS WAKE*
(Madison: University of Wisconsin Press, 1986)

This book keeps firmly in focus the concept that *Finnegans Wake* is a reconstruction of dream-consciousness. By drawing on Freud, Vico, Egyptian beliefs about death, and detailed etymological accounts, Bishop explains how Joyce created a language of wilful obscurity using dream phenomena, metahistorical theories and the intricacies of word formation. On this basis, the author asserts that Joyce composed the quirky night-world of *Finnegans Wake* as an anti-universe which undermines the concept of a universe based on scientific investigation. Thus Bishop's book addresses the question of whether, as a writer, Joyce is a scientific rationalist, as some critics believe, or a chronicler of basically anarchic forces of the physical and mental worlds.

Articles and Chapters in Books

J39   Connolly, Cyril
"The Position of Joyce", *Life and Letters* (1929), pp. 273–90; also in THE CONDEMNED PLAYGROUND: ESSAYS: 1927–1944 (London: Routledge, 1945; New York: Macmillan, 1946), pp. 1–15

An early reaction to the "Anna Livia Plurabelle" section of "Work in Progress". This essay, written by an informed critic, starts with a discussion of *Ulysses* and provides a lucid general statement on Joyce's position in modern letters. Connolly stresses the importance of Joyce's experimental language, his interest in Irish myth and history, and his single-minded devotion to literature.

J40   Edel, Leon
"James Joyce and His New Work", *University of Toronto Quarterly*, 9 (1939), 68–81

Considers Joyce's art as composed with the delicate interaction of ear and eye to the point that only Joyce's reading aloud of the work would convey the tonal richness of his language.

J41   Ransom, John Crowe
"The Aesthetic of *Finnegans Wake*", *Kenyon Review*, 1 (1939), 424–8

Views *Finnegans Wake* as an intense reactionary response to the predominant scientific mentality of the age. Ransom's short piece encapsulates the sentiment of many American critics toward *Finnegans Wake* upon its initial reception in America.

J42   Richardson, Dorothy
        "Adventure for Readers", *Life and Letters Today*, 22 (July
        1939), 45–52

        A subjective response to reading *Finnegans Wake* by a noted
        experimental novelist. Richardson defends the obscurity of the
        book and draws attention to the "Anna Livia Plurabelle"
        chapter as example of Joyce's ability to be imaginative,
        moving and also clear.

J43   Troy, William
        "Notes on *Finnegans Wake*", *Partisan Review*, 6 (1939),
        97–110

        This brief insightful response to the publication of the
        complete *Finnegans Wake* discusses the musicality of Joyce's
        language; punning and synecdoche as rhetorical devices;
        parallels with Vico, Jung and Einstein; and the use of dream
        structure as a principle of narration. Troy also defends Joyce
        against American Marxist critics who saw Joyce's work and
        modernism in general as too subjective and removed from the
        class struggle. (Reprinted in D6.)

J44   Wilson, Edmund L.
        "The Dream of H. C. Earwicker", (1939), THE WOUND
        AND THE BOW (New York: Oxford University Press,
        1947), pp. 243–71

        Based upon his *New Republic* reviews of 28 June and 11 July
        1939, this piece constitutes the most important of the early
        reactions to the work. Wilson's criticism of *Finnegans Wake*
        reflects the dilemma of many critics who admired *Finnegans
        Wake* but were concerned with Joyce's isolation from
        contemporary concerns. (Reprinted in D6 and D108.)

J45   Bishop, John Peale
        "*Finnegans Wake*" (1940), THE COLLECTED ESSAYS OF
        JOHN PEALE BISHOP, ed. Edmund Wilson (New York:
        Scribner's, 1948), pp. 146–65

        An appreciation of *Finnegans Wake* through the sensibility of
        a poet. Bishop stresses Joyce's almost complete break with the
        realism of Flaubert, his riddle-like transformations of

language and thought, and his sublimation of the personal to the universal cycle of history.

J46   Chase, Richard V.
"*Finnegans Wake*: An Anthropological Study", *American Scholar*, 13 (1944), 418–26

An extravagant appraisal of *Finnegans Wake* as a modern version of the Bible with other parallels to the writings of the historian A. J. Toynbee and the nineteenth-century anthropologist James Frazer.

J47   Glasheen, Adaline
"*Finnegans Wake* and the Girls from Boston, Mass.", *Hudson Review*, 7 (1954), 89–96

Speculates on a third woman in *Finnegans Wake* in addition to Anna Livia and Issy. Glasheen draws a parallel between a book Joyce may have read on the dissociation of a female personality and the split character of Issy.

J48   Atherton, James S

"*Finnegans Wake*: 'The Gist of Pantomime'", *Accent*, 15 (1955), 14–26

Explores the *Wake* in terms of the conventions of British pantomime. By referring to the *Wake* notebook in the British Museum, the author shows how Joyce took a children's story or nursery rhyme and submerged such a core under the standard devices of a pantomime act: puns, jokes, dances, song and topical gags.

J49   Peter, John
"Joyce and the Novel", *Kenyon Review*, 18 (1956), 619–32

Argues that Joyce has undermined the novel form by withdrawing from the immediacy of human experience into the remote and mythological. Peter asserts that any enthusiasm for *Finnegans Wake* can only be based on unverifiable acts of faith.

J50   *The Analyst*, Nos 10, 12, 15–17, 19–24 (1956–65)

A series of articles are offered devoted to commentary on and addenda to Joyce's works. Number 20 contains John Kelleher's "Notes on *Finnegans Wake* and *Ulysses*"; number 23 contains a paraphrase of the end of *Finnegans Wake* by John Hensdale Thompsen and additional notes by Kelleher. The remaining issues contain a good deal of annotated information, all devoted to aspects of *Ulysses* and *Finnegans Wake*, from Fritz Senn, Adaline Glasheen and Ruth von Phul.

J51   Hayman, David
        "Dramatic Motion in *Finnegans Wake*", *Texas Studies in English*, 37 (1958), 155–76

A discussion of how Joyce used thematic materials in the elaboration of the first draft of the "Butt and Tail" skit, "How Buckley Shot the Russian General". This examination of draft materials discusses how dramatic intensity in the *Wake* is achieved by the fusing of several planes of experience into a simultaneous moment. Yet although these coexisting planes operate within the same narrative moment, they also retain a variable effect that applies to the overall context of the *Wake* as well as a particular moment of reading.

J52   Hayman, David
        "From *Finnegans Wake*: A Sentence in Progress", *PMLA*, 73 (1958), 136–54

Examines the permutations of a single sentence based on his study of all extant manuscripts. Hayman's demonstration reveals a great deal about Joyce's techniques generally as well as his overall method in the construction of *Finnegans Wake*.

J53   *Wake Newslitter*, 1 (March 1962), 18 (December 1963); new series, 1 (February 1964), 17 (December 1980) (1962–1980)

A publication which contains brief studies of *Finnegans Wake* and other related items. Most of these notes reflect close textual examination of sources of Joyce. The explications have an accretive value along with their individual insights. After the *Newslitter* was discontinued in 1980, it was continued in part by *A Wake Newslitter: Occasional Paper*.

J54   Wilder, Thornton
       "Giordano Bruno's Last Meal in *Finnegans Wake*", *Hudson Review*, 16 (1963), 74–9

       Discusses the simultaneous multivalent associations in a single passage from the *Wake* with particular emphasis on the trial and execution of Giordano Bruno. This essay is especially interesting in that, besides its immediate insights, it reveals Wilder's larger method for reading *Finnegans Wake*.

J55   Benstock, Bernard
       "Every Telling Has a Taling: A Reading of the Narrative of *Finnegans Wake*", *Modern Fiction Studies*, 15 (1969), 3–25

       An excellent consideration of the narrative problems in the *Wake*. The author traces with care the narrative line which he contends brings unity to the work.

J56   Barrett, William
       "Myth or the Museum?", TIME OF NEED: FORMS OF IMAGINATION IN THE TWENTIETH CENTURY (New York: Harper and Row, 1972), pp. 312–50

       Argues that despite a highly experimental style, Joyce is a traditional anti-modern writer in terms of content. This is not a new argument, but Barrett's essay builds on the concerns which were often expressed in early criticism of *Finnegans Wake*, especially in America.

J57   Begnal, Michael H.
       "James Joyce and the Mythologizing of History", DIRECTIONS IN LITERARY CRITICISM: CONTEMPORARY APPROACHES TO LITERATURE, ed. Stanley Weintraub and Philip Young (University Park: Pennsylvania State University Press, 1973), pp. 211–19.

       Examines several bodies of myth which Joyce incorporated into *Finnegans Wake*, asserting that Joyce's primary impulse was the creation through past mythical structures of a modern myth.

J58   Polhemus, Robert M.
       "Joyce's *Finnegans Wake* (1924–39): The Comic Gospel of

'Shem'", COMIC FAITH: THE GREAT TRADITION
FROM AUSTEN TO JOYCE (Chicago: University of
Chicago Press, 1980), pp. 294–337

Focusing on the comical "Shem" section of *Finnegans Wake*,
the author proceeds to relate Joyce to other British comic
writers such as Dickens, Thackeray, Meredith and Carroll.
This comic tradition is seen as a mode of criticizing and
undermining established religious dogma.

J59   Sukenick, Ronald
       "Endless Short Story: The Finnegan Digression", *Sub-stance*,
       27 (1980), 3–6

An experimental novelist recreates the language of the *Wake*
through a tandem narration, which retells the story of Anna
Livia Plurabelle while interpreting it at the same time.

J60   Devlin, Kimberley
       "Self and Other in *Finnegans Wake*: A Framework for
       Analyzing Versions of Shem and Shaun", *James Joyce
       Quarterly* 21:1 (Fall 1983), 31–50

This article begins by briefly surveying how Joyce, before
Finnegans Wake, based his characters upon a pattern of
conflict between an internal self and an external authority,
usually a literary antecedent. The author then distinguishes
characterization in *Finnegans Wake* from Joyce's preceding
works, describing how the pattern of conflict is completely
internalized as different aspects of a single dreaming
consciousness.

Index of Contributors

This index includes authors, editors and compilers of works that appear as entries in this bibliography as well as authors of essays who are mentioned in annotations for collected works and special issues.

Adams, Robert M.: A4, D28, D60, H7, I11
Aitken, D. J. F.: D149, H5
Allott, Miriam: I93
Almeida, Hermione de: I49
Anderson, Chester G.: B28, D98, D139, G2, G8, G14, G20, I24
Anderson, Elliott: J27
Anderson, Margaret: B2
Andreach, Robert J.: G28
apRoberts, Robert P.: F42
Atherton, James S.: F5, G29, J4, J11, J48
Attridge, Derek: D97
Aubert, Jacques: D50, D97, D156
August, Eugene: G7

Baker, James R.: D121, E2, F3, F22
Barrett, William: J56
Barrow, Craig Wallace: I44
Bates, Ronald: D44, J11
Bauerle, Ruth: H13, I89
Beach, Joseph Warren: I69
Beach, Sylvia: B22, B33
Beck, Warren: F4
Beckett, Samuel: B32, D108, J1, J27
Beebe, Maurice: A8, D44, G11, G22, G47, I32
Begnal, Michael H.: D44, D98, J19, J21, J57
Beja, Morris: D136, D156, F9, G11, G40
Bekker, Peter: D89
Benco, Silvio: B3, B37
Benstock, Bernard: A13, D58, D61, D72, D80, D81, D98, D107, D108, D151, D154, D158, D164, F5, F43, F64, G14, G45, H10, I19, I30, J8, J11, J19, J55
Benstock, Shari: D72, D85, D108, D143
Bidwell, Bruce: F11, G16
Bierman, Robert: D149
Bigazzi, Carlo: D102
Bishop, John: J38, J45
Blackmur, R. P.: I75
Blamires, Harry: I13
Blissett, William: D32
Bluefarb, Sam: D154
Boldereff, Frances M.: J5
Bonheim, Helmut: J12
Bonnerot, Louis: I27
Booth, Wayne C.: G8, G11, G26
Bosinelli, Rosa Maria: D115
Bowen, Zack: D53, D98, D100, D158, E4, F5, I28
Boyd, Elizabeth F.: G24
Boyle, Robert, S. J.: D66, D83, D85, D93, D100, F2, F5, F24, F48, I30, I86, J19
Bradley, Bruce, S. J.: B41
Brandabur, Edward: D45
Bremen, Brian A.: F74
Brivic, Sheldon: D73, D93, D163
Broch, Hermann: B12, D118
Broes, Arthur T.: J17
Brown, Homer Obed: G10
Brown, Norman O.: D100
Brown, Richard: D109
Buckley, Jerome H.: G43
Budgen, Frank: B4, B30, B33, D6, D108, J1, J10
Burgan, Mary: I111
Burgess, Anthony: D27, D51, F9
Burke, Kenneth: G30
Bushrui, Suheil Badi: D81
Butor, Michel: D156
Buttigieg, Joseph A.: G17
Byrne, John Francis: B15